WORKING MEDIA WOMEN
Profile, Work Environment and Job Satisfaction

WORKING MEDIA WOMEN
Profile, Work Environment and Job Satisfaction

D.V.R. Murthy
G. Anita

KANISHKA PUBLISHERS, DISTRIBUTORS
NEW DELHI-110 002

KANISHKA PUBLISHERS, DISTRIBUTORS
4697/5-21 A, Ansari Road, Daryaganj
New Delhi-110 002
Phones : 2327 0497, 2328 8285
Fax : 011-2328 8285
E-mail: kanishka_publishing@yahoo.co.in

Working Media Women:
Profile, Work Environment and Job Satisfaction

First Published 2009

ISBN 978-81-8457-148-6

PRINTED IN INDIA

Published by Madan Sachdeva for Kanishka Publishers, Distributors, 4697/5-21A, Ansari Road, Daryaganj, New Delhi-110 002, Typeset by Sunshine Graphics, Delhi, and Printed at Rajdhani Printers, Delhi.

PREFACE

With the proliferation of news channels in the country, the work force has correspondingly grown in the country. In India, Jeffrey (2000) estimated that there were 4700 journalists in early 1960's and around 13,000 in 1990's. In the year 1990's India had about 25,000 journalists on wages or retainers, which came up to one journalist for every 35,000 people. This excluded thousands of stringers and contributors. Although the work force is increasingly going up, very few studies have been conducted to examine the sociological issues involved in the career of media men or women. However, a few studies that are available in the country have focused on the media men or media women who are working in the print media. Unlike the earlier studies, the present study has attempted to study the sociological issues of media women who include print journalists, television anchors, script writers, and radio announcers. The study has been conducted in Andhra Pradesh, a state which has witnessed a media boom in the recent years.

In fact, the study was done in 2007 by covering three cities in Andhra Pradesh-Hyderabad, Vijayawada and Visakhapatnam. At the time of data collection, there were few television channels, and hence few respondents represented them. Further, in any survey research, data collection poses a problem in view of the non-availability and non-cooperation of the respondents. In the present study too, senior journalists refused to fill the questionnaire as soon as they read the questionnaire. Nevertheless, about 130 media women filled the questionnaire with many reminders. We thank all those respondents who cooperated with us in making the study. We also thank the reviewers for their comments to improve the manuscript. We thank all those people who helped us directly and indirectly in completing the study.

D.V.R. Murthy
G. Anita

CONTENTS

1

WOMEN AND MEDIA

In ancient India, women were venerated owing to the country's traditional and cultural diversity. During the different periods in the history of the country, women were given an elevated status, but they were not given an equal status on a par with men. However, with the appointment of the national committee on the status of women in India in 1972, and the publication of its report in 1975 marked the first official attempt in contemporary times to study the status of women in India and recommend changes to improve their position. The report highlighted that despite constitutional guarantees the roles, rights and participation of women in all spheres of life were limited (Ghadially, 1988). Yet, transition in the pattern of employment of middle and upper class women especially married women changed this trend. This resulted in the enhancement of status of women in the society, and there were many influences that led to this enhancement of the status. Entry of women into the labour force is one such influence that has effected changes in the status of the women. The notable consequences are family life, marital relationships, corporate income and childcare (Vijaya Lakshmi and Devi Prasad, 1999). In spite of the entry of women into the labour force, and the women becoming self-reliant, the status of women in terms of being considered an equal partner in the work is not gaining importance in the family and the workplace. For example, women typically receive lower pay than men even when they work in the same sector.

After 60 years of Independence in India, although the growth is commendable in some sectors, the social problems are still looming large. However great is the contribution of women to the nation they still do not get their due share of recognition, equality and empathy. Studies say that the number of working women in India is constantly changing and they are entering into the new fields which are so far untrodden by women. This trend is positive, but gender inequalities remain pervasive in many dimensions of life. While disparities exist throughout the world, they are most prevalent in poor developing countries. According to ILO report (2002), the labour force gender parity index for the world has remained the same at 0.7 over the last decade between 1990 and 2000. It has also been observed that the index is lowest for Middle East and North Africa at 0.4, followed by South Asia at 0.5. The same index is highest for Europe and Central Asia at 0.9 for the year 2000.

In India, the 2001 census reported the number of working women was 127.04 million out of a total female population of 494.82 million. This included 72.65 million main workers and 54.39 million female marginal workers. On classifying women workers into rural and urban categories, it emerged that 60.33 million women were working as main workers in rural areas in comparison to 12.31 million in urban areas. Similarly 51.11 million female marginal workers worked in rural areas and only 3.27 million in urban areas. Thus, there were as many as 367.78 million non-workers among the women in the year 2001 (Mathur, 2007).

In India, the comparative data for 1911 recorded 41.8 million female workers out of a total female population of 123.8 million only (Prabhash P. Singh (1991) cited in Mathur, 2007). Thus the percentage of women workers in the total work force declined from 34.44 per cent in 1911 to 23.19 per cent in 2001. Another alarming feature is the continuous decline in the low work force participation among women. The work participation rate declined from 33.7 per cent in 1911 to 14.68 in 2001. The work participation rate in 2001 is lower than the corresponding figure of 15.93 in 1991. In fact, this declining trend in the proportion of female workers has continued over the decades (See Table 1).

Table–1
Trends in Employment of Women in India 1911-2001

Year [a]	*Total Female Workers (in million)*	*Work Participation Rate*[b] *(WPR) %*	*Female Workers to Total Workers %*
1911	41.802	33.73	34.44
1921	40.095	32.66	34.02
1931	37.600	27.63	31.17
1951	40.539	23.30	28.98
1961	59.402	27.96	31.53
1971	31.298	11.86	17.35
1981	44.973	13.99	20.21
1991	64.273	15.93	22.47
2001	72.652	14.68	23.19

Note: *(a)* Figures of 1941 census are not available.
(b) Workers include only main workers; Work Participation Rate (WPR) means female workers to total female population.

Source: Mathur, Kalpana (2007), Human Potential: A Case Study of Female Economic Activity in India. *International Journal for Women and Gender Research*, 1 (1): 30-34.

Although 1980s have witnessed an increase in employment of women, several social scientists pointed out that the ramifications of Structural Adjustment Programmes (SAP) hit the women workforce more gravely in some sectors. This is because a large percentage of women are in the organized sector which is subjected to downsizing through voluntary retirement scheme (Shah *et al.*, 1994: 42; Jha and Pujari 1996).

Nevertheless, the demand for women workers is on the increase everywhere in the world (Swarajya Laxmi, 1992). They have been trying to accept the chances of employment and empower themselves with economic independence and prove their worth in societies. In this course of identifying themselves as equal contributors to the family's development many a time they had to compromise on home front. They had to balance between their careers and family lives. However, a large percentage of working women still continue to pursue their conventional family arrangement by adjusting their working hours to their family responsibilities rather than the reverse as men do (Voydanoff, 1993).

Women, Family and Childcare

With the advent of the globalization, the empowerment of women has been on the rise and has impacted the family structure. The joint family system which has been in vogue in India for many years has been increasingly undergoing a change, and the nuclear family system of two or three members has come into place. Thus, Devi Prasad (1996) has observed that the changes in Indian family structure can be examined from two different angles. They are the effect of socio-economic changes on the family structure, demographic features, and the second one, the consequence of these changes on family functions and family life. Further, he observed that the socio-economic changes primarily affected the family in the areas of marital quality, women's employment, family life, family and healthcare.

Added to this, the employment of the women in the family has affected the childcare. Researchers observe that childcare is a conceptually distinct and especially burdensome aspect of household work (Berk, 1985; Rextrot and Shahan, 1987), and residential nurseries (Bledsoe and Isingo–Abanihe, 1989; Nelson, 1987). Moreover, 'childcare is increasingly becoming a major problem for the dual earner families' (Goldscheider and Waite, 1991).

Billings and Moos (1982) and Repetti (1987) examined that an employed woman would find lesser time and opportunity to spend time with her husband thus causing stress and reasons contributing to negative marital adjustment. Therefore it may be said that pressure at work may bring about disillusionment and cause moods resulting in negative marital interactions (Crouter *et al.*, 1989; Repetti, 1989). Further, Voydanoff (1988) saw that increased work hours had a direct negative effect on family conflict. Furthermore, Kingston and Nack (1987) reported that family-time for recreation, entertainment, watching TV, eating meals together was notably structured by the number of working hours expended in paid work. As Mickelson and Smith (1992) note, using a metaphor, if life is a game, the playing field must be leveled; if life is a race, the starting line must be in the same place for every one. Slowly the lines are being drawn from the same distance for both the genders.

While research in Western societies exclusively dealt with the dilemmas of working families into the social environment (Berk, 1985; Rapoport and Rapoport 1982; Aldous, 1982), studies taken up in India have explored issues such as women's reasons for entering paid employment, division of house work, impact of mother's work on childcare, gender roles, decision making in the family etc. (Banerjee, 1989; Chakrabarthy, 1978; Devi, 1987).

Women and Sexual Harassment

In response to the first United Nations World Conference on women in December 1975 at Mexico, a national plan of action for women was adopted in 1976. Subsequent International Women's Conference viz., Copenhagen in 1980, Nairobi in 1985 and Beijing in 1995 emphasized the role of mass media in the elimination of gender inequality and sexual harassment. However, some international efforts at institutionalization of gender mainstreaming coupled with the Supreme Court's guidelines in India on sexual harassment at the workplace in 1997 mandated organizations to address sexual harassment[1] at the workplace in India. The Committee Against Sexual Harassment (CASH) was formed in 1998 mainly to address and prevent sexual harassment at the workplace in India. Very soon the Committee started looking at other gender issues at workplace. Women are hesitant to report incidents of sexual harassment since they feel that no action is taken against the perpetrator. Addressing sexual harassment for safe working environment, most civil society organizations as well as government organizations deny the existence of sexual harassment within those sectors. Yet it remains a reality. Incidents of sexual harassment are largely not reported since there is no enabling environment within the organization for its reporting (Saxena and Thekkudan, 2007). Although many countries appear to have laws or policies against unequal pay and sex discrimination, many of these laws are vaguely worded and in most cases it appears that their effectiveness has not been evaluated. Such policies appear to have little impact on deeply entrenched patterns of inequality, and numerous obstacles to the successful enforcement of policy were reported in the questionnaires.

Women and Media

The UNESCO studies indicate that throughout the world much more is known about images of women than about women's participation in media industries. In general, employment data on women and media around the world are incomplete and unreliable (Seager and Olson, 1986; UNESCO, 1985, 1989).

Despite these observations, UNESCO study (1989) shows that around the world the proportion of women journalism students greatly exceeds the proportion of women working in journalism. These statistics likely forecast a growing number of women in journalism professions globally, though these women continue to face many discouraging obstacles. In addition, Cooper (1988) reports that at least in some ways women may be making more progress in some Third world media. But, studies in Japan, the United States, Colombia, Jamaica, and Sri Lanka indicate that women have a more prominent role as reporters and anchors. She did observe a bias against women as foreign correspondents in all five countries as well as an apparent universal tendency to assign women to cover only domestic issues.

Seager and Olson (1986) were able to report simple data on proportions of women in the media workforce from only

46 countries and on both print and broadcast media from only 25. Their data indicate that women made up more than 30 per cent of the total media work force in Costa Rica, Chile, Taiwan, Venezuela (35%) and in Cuba, Thailand, and the United States (40%). Women made up 5 per cent or less of the media work force in Bangladesh (1%), Peru and Japan (2%) and Haiti and Honduras (5%). Countries that reported only broadcast media data reported 30 per cent or more women in the work force in Sweden (30%), Singapore (38%), and Jamaica (50%), and less than 5 per cent in Australia (0%), Austria (2%), Ghana (3%) and Norway (4%). Just as China is fast emerging as the super power in many fields the statistics in media are also progressive. Women now account for 41 per cent of total media work force in China.

According to Margaret Gallagher (1995), women are not a significant part of the media work force. In Asia women are 21 per cent of the total media work force. In South Africa they are 27 per cent. In Western Europe and the United States they are 35 per cent. Worldwide women are 79 per cent of all part time workers in the news media. In Japan, women are only 8 per cent of media employees, in India and Malawi, they are 12 per cent and in Argentina and Mozambique, women are 16 per cent of the media work force. In Africa, women are 8 per cent of the broadcasting managers and 14 per cent mangers in the print media. In Latin America, the figures are 21 per cent for broadcasting and 16 per cent for print.

Ahmar (2004), analyzed the participation and position of women in the Pakistani Media and the impact of those positions on women's development. She noted that in the 54-year history of Pakistan, no woman had ever been editor of an Urdu newspaper and only two women had been editors of English daily. New private television and radio channels have employed young women as reporters and DJs, but that is where it all stops. In Saudi Arabia, the situation is no different. "Ten years ago when I started, people used to be surprised if a woman journalist turned up to report anywhere," said Rima al-Shamikh (2004) a news anchor with al-Ikhbariya who reported from the field during the violent campaign launched by Al-Qaeda sympathizers in 2003 to bring down the Saudi monarchy.

Minority representation in American Media has increased over the years, but, at 9.5 per cent by 2002, remained much below the minority percentage of the U.S. population and also the college-educated minority population. The percentage of African Americans in full-time reporting positions has remained static from 1971 to 2002, from 3.9 per cent to 3.7 per cent (Gallagher, 1981).

For instance, Gallagher (1981) found that throughout the world women were virtually absent from top executive positions and at the lower level women were segregated into lower paying clerical occupations. The few news positions typically handled traditional women's features and less important assignments.

Other problems discussed by Gallagher (1981) include job conditions assuming male roles (e.g., the expectations of high performance in youth with no consideration for child bearing and childcare), women's poor record of active union membership, protective legislation for media women (e.g., laws in some countries restricting overtime and night work for women) and inadequate training and education for women in media. In broadcasting media, Gallagher (1981) notes women's minority presence, women's absence from technical jobs and senior management and women's segregation into certain programme making areas such as educational and children's programmes.

Women in Indian Media

Soon after the Independence, most of the media organizations were owned by Indian businessmen, and the majority of the employees were Indians. Mostly, the newspapers are in the private sector and the government-controlled radio and the television. Moreover, the newspapers used to employ only men on the ground that the men could be deputed to different kinds of work while posting them for the night shift. Thus, women were not employed till 1960s. The typical experience of a woman journalist is reflected in a statement of Usha Rai, a noted journalist in the country. Usha Rai (2003) writes:

> When I joined the *Times of India*, Delhi, in 1964 there was not a single woman on the editorial section of the newspaper. There was no woman in the reporting unit, on the desk or the edit page. The only women in the newspaper were receptionists and telephone operators. There was no toilet for women on the editorial floor and I had to get to the telephone operators to borrow the key to use their toilet on the ground floor.

'Many a time the patriarchal nature of men journalists translates into discrimination and harassment, stereotyped attitudes, sexual harassment, salary differences, unfair treatment in assignments and promotions, traditional gender biases and lack of support mechanisms for working women deter women from joining the media or assuming decision making positions' (Bhavani and Vijaya Lakshmi, 2005). Usha Rai (2003) also shares almost the same view. Majority of women journalists are forced to confine to desk which are claimed to be safe and secure resulting in more number of sub-editors. The Press Institute of India Report (2004) observed that though an increasing number of women are entering the reporting field the nature of the reporting they do is definitely not encouraging. The gender discrimination is evident in the way beats and coverage of stories is assigned. Women still are limited to assignments of "soft issues" such as fashions, culture, arts, and life style while men are assigned political and economic stories, which are considered more as "hard issues."

Sociological Study of Gender and Work

In the context of studying gender-specific issues, researchers have taken up studies related to workplace differences between males and females. Most studies of this phenomenon have aimed at determining whether men and women in similar occupations differ on a variety of factors such as style of working (Table 2).

Table–2
Gender and Working Styles

Feminine	*Masculine*
Indirect	Direct
Conciliatory	Confrontational
Facilitative	Competitive
Collaborative	Autonomous
Minor contribution (in public)	Dominates talking time (in time)
Supportive feedback	Aggressive interpretations
Person/process oriented	Task/outcome oriented
Affectively oriented	Referentially oriented

Source: Holmes, J. and Stubbe, M. (2003). Feminine workplaces: Stereotype and reality. In J. Holmes and M. Meyerhoff (eds.), *The handbook of language and gender* (pp. 573-599). Malden, MA; Oxford.

The assumption guiding this body of research is that women bring different values and view points to the workplace that can serve as a resource for change. Applied to the news profession; however, research examining male and female reporting differences have been inconclusive (Rodgers and Thorson, 2003). Neverthless, two competing models of socialization offer a framework for understanding the inconclusive findings on reporting differences and gender– the gender model and the job model (Rodgers and Thorson, 2003).

Gender Model

Dodd-McCue and Wright (1996) observe that the gender model points out that men and women socialize differently into the workplace because men and women have different values and priorities. Because women are assumed to value interdependent, nurturing relationships (Cook, 1993) with priorities that emphasize family values and roles (Kinnier, *et al.*, 1991), while men are presumed to value independent, assertive and goal-directed behaviour (Cook, 1993) with priorities that relate to self perception and self promotion (Aven *et al.*, 1993). However, other studies indicate that men and women have different moral thinking (Grant, 1988), different gender-linked language (Mulac, *et al.*, 2001) and 'different work interests and concerns' (Bertz and O'Connell, 1989). 'Women also relate differently to people than men and advocate more democracy, less hierarchy, and more cooperation than their male counterparts' (Bertz and O'Connell, 1989). Further, different gender orientations affect the manner in which males and females learn to behave and carry out their jobs (ex., socialize) in the workplace (Aven *et al.*, 1993). This approach leads to an important argument for the recruitment of female reporters or journalists into male-dominated newsrooms. The argument is that women represent values and working methods from which news organizations will profit, for example, by improving the amount and type of coverage that women receive (Beasley, 1989). Female reporters, like females in other professions are expected to bring the manner in which news stories are researched, framed and written.

Job Model

Contrary to the gender model, the job model contends that socialization is a function of the work environment (Aven *et al.*, 1993). Under this model, women are assumed to perform the same as men to the extent that their organizational experiences are similar. Thus, organizations with male dominated power structures and political climates may promote social interactions in which female employees are expected to avoid exclusion or gain promotion. The job model points out that woman in male dominated professions such as news reporting might develop the same attitude and behaviours as men in the same profession (Terborg, 1977). Thus, the job model predicts that the reporting of male and female journalists may differ in news rooms where a highest concentration of female reporters/editors exists. A larger number of female journalists will presumably change the power structure, politics, and organization of newsroom thereby giving females a greater freedom and confidence to report the news in ways that are more consistent with critical social habits ingrained since childhood. Having a higher proportion of female reporters and editors should subsequently challenge a power system where males not only comprise the majority but also create and maintain the political climate of the newsroom, thus leading to grater differences between male and female reporting (Rodgers and Thorson, 2003).

The size of a newspaper is the second organizational factor presumed to affect the socialization process of male and female reporters and subsequent news stories written and framed by these reporters. Soloski (1989) has identified a newspaper's size as a factor contributing to a reporter's selection of sources and frames used to construct and represent reality in news coverage (Altheide, 1976).

Previous Studies

The sociological study of mass communicators has received less attention as compared to research on content, impact of audience, and inferred effects of mass communication. However, in the recent past, interest on examining the sociological aspects of mass communicators has grown, and various studies related to status and role, occupational problems, analyses of complex organizations and so on have been taken up in different settings. In the following pages, studies dealing with journalists' background, job satisfaction, and nature of job and others with particular reference to women have been presented.

United States of America (USA)

In the USA large numbers of studies were conducted on journalists, specifically focused on the socio-demographic profile (Johnstone *et al.*, 1976), job satisfaction (Beam, 2006), working conditions (Miller and Miller, 1995) and sexual harassment of women journalists (Walsh-Childers *et al.*, 1997). For example Johnstone *et al.*, (1976) studied the socio-demographic details of the journalists. The study found that nearly 4 out of 5 journalists were directly engaged in reporting, newsgathering and news writing while 7 out of 10 edited or processed other people's work and 4 out of 10 had managerial and supervisor duties. The proportions that do news reporting regularly tend to decrease with several years of experience in the media.

In relation to television, Gitlin (1983) examined the process of television production through personal observations and interviews with more than 200 television producers, network executives, writers, actors, and agents in the 1980s. He discussed how television shows were affected by interpersonal, economic, political, and other considerations.

About radio, Smith and Harwood study (1996) found that women of 28 years age entered radio by "chance "and worked in the medium on an average of 3 to 4 years. Men, on the other hand, trained for the radio profession and worked in the field for 10 to 14 years. More than a fourth of the women and 47 per cent men surveyed cited money and career advancement as reasons for leaving their last positions. Interestingly, only a quarter of the women cited family and personal considerations as reasons for leaving their last positions.

Women Work Force in Media

Women's presence throughout the male professions grew from the late nineteenth century through the 1920's, but their presence was most greatly felt in journalism. In 1920, 5730 women were among 34,197 reporters and editors (16.75% counted in the census by 1940). In a 1917 survey conducted by the Federal Bureau of Vocations, 51 newspaper women interviewed were unwilling to admit or perceive sex discrimination. Although 47 answered the question about their duties, only 27 answered a query about whether they had experienced sex discrimination and only 12 compared women's and men's chances to be assigned to the "big" story (Cott, 1987). Next, Lumsden (1995) studied the concept of gender and women journalists in the 1920s and 1930s. The study demonstrated how gender based polarities affected 10 front-page gals "between 1920 and 1940." It demonstrates how women journalists had to lose their feminine selves to succeed in the male dominated city room. The study said that the women's emphasis on succeeding on individual merit left them unable to recognize structural discrimination in pay, assignments, and benefits. Women journalists, like other professionals of the era, were so intent upon personal fulfillment they failed to recognize how the male *status quo* benefited by ridiculing women who challenged it. However, Ware (1982) found out that for women journalists: "any weakness is likely to be considered feminine. According to Ware, "newspaper women in the 1920's and 1930's had to act as tough as Superman while working but blend demurely into the wall paper after deadline." For instance, *New York Times* allowed no woman reporter in the city room until 1934. However, Scott (1986) argued that women journalists apparently learned the lesson well, as their words strikingly illustrate the conflicting pressures created by a polarized view of what constitute male and female characteristics. In some instances, instead of uniting in a collective struggle, the reporters dealt individually with discrimination, striving to prove their worth solely through their work. Even among professional women, the women reporters comprised elite. Only a quarter of all women worked, and out of them only 14.2 per cent worked as professionals in 1930. Most of them worked as teachers or nurses. Further the idea of combining marriage and career remained novel in the 1920's, only 19.3 per cent of professional women married in 1920, a figure that rose to 24.7 per cent in 1930. Interestingly, seven of the 10 women in this study married at least once, illustrating Cott's contention that the attempt to combine marriage and career was a professional women's statement of autonomy.

Newspapers were opted by women for several reasons: Journalism was more open partly because the field had resisted rigid professionalization, unlike law and medicine, which limited women through strict admissions quotas to professional schools and omitted them from crucial internships. Elite universities such as Harvard and Yale banned women altogether. In contrast, as early as the nineteenth century a limited number of women found a niche in literature and journalism because writing and editing involved training and discipline that was largely individual and could be acquired in the private sphere (Flexner, 1975). Even, the Maryland report in 1985 (cited in Beasley, 1989) concluded that women were making an impact on the male dominated field of journalism but they encountered far more obstacles than men in advancing to the top. Indeed women graduates appeared to experience somewhat more difficulty than male graduates in finding journalism related jobs including those on daily newspapers. In the mid 1980s women students perceived greater potential for discrimination in the workplace than men although all recognized the presence of discrimination on the basis of sex. Women agreed more strongly than men with a statement on the questionnaire that women doing journalism related work were lower paid than men doing comparable work. They also agreed more strongly with a statement that a man would be hired over an equally capable woman (Beasly and Theus, 1988). In Weaver *et al.*, study (2006) it was found out that 64 per cent of the students enrolled in US Universities were women in journalism programmes. The study also found out that there was an increase of women journalists in 2002 in the youngest age group. Women made up 60 per cent in the less than 25 years age group in journalism work force and women reached more than 40 per cent in the age group of 25-34. The study also noted that beyond the age of 35 the percentage of women remained low and there was a drop both in 35-44 and 45-54 age groups. In this study it was found in 2002 that women with experience of 5-9 years group consisted of 41.2 per cent while 34.4 per cent were in the 10-14 years group and 25 per cent in 15-19 years group. Interestingly the study found out that 100 per cent of women remain unmarried but living with a partner. Nearly a third of women (32.5%) said that they had children living at home which is an increase of 5 per cent from the earlier study conducted in 1992.

A large percentage of working women still continue to pursue their conventional family arrangement by adjusting their working hours to their family responsibilities rather than the reverse as men do (Voydanoff, 1993). In fact, a study of journalists in the Washington Press Corps commissioned by the American Women in Journalism revealed that at the uppermost levels of the profession even marriage appears to be antithetical to women's success.

A number of studies of women in journalism have also found that they are less likely than men in the field to be married or to have children (Beasley and Theus, 1988; Goodrick, 1989; Lafky, 1991; Ogan *et al.*, 1979).

Journalism Education and Career

Although women tend to predominate in journalism undergraduate and graduate programmes by a 60/40 ratio, once on the job, they seem to have an eye on putting it aside for a while, if not permanently. American Society of Newspapers Editors survey revealed that only 34 per cent of the women planned to stay in journalism until their 60s, as compared to 48 per cent of the men. And 55 per cent of the women aged 30 and under said they would leave journalism before turning 40, as opposed to 32 per cent of the 30-and under men (Gallaghar, 1981).

Women once again composed of 60 per cent of the students at undergraduate and graduate journalism programmes, according to a 1996 enrollment survey published by the Association for Education in Journalism and Mass Communication. Undergraduates have been at this level since 1968; graduates since 1988. And while many of the journalism schools in the survey include predominantly female mass communication and advertising sequences, even the strictly journalistic graduate programme at Columbia University reports the number of women students ranging from 58 to 66 per cent over the past four years (Gallagher, 1981). According to Potter (1988), more than half of the US journalists are under the age of 35 years and only 10 per cent are 55 years or older. Potter says that almost all of the US journalists have a college degree.

Sexual Harassment

The US courts have recognized two categories of sexual harassment, known as *"quid pro quo"* ("something for something") and "hostile environment" discrimination (Walsh-Childers *et al.*, 1997). The former refers to situations in which an individual promises a subordinate employee some sort of tangible job benefit, such as a raise in exchange for sexual favours. This category also likely would include more negatively stated interactions, such as a supervisor's threat that the victim will lose her job if she refuses the supervisor's request for sexual favours. The latter, "hostile environment" discrimination, reflects circumstances in which an employee is subjected to a pattern of behaviour-such as unwanted sexual advances, degrading sexual comments about the employee of similar problems - that infers unreasonably with an employee's ability to perform his or her job or makes the workplace environment inhospitable, intimidating or offensive.

Newspaper women often report that sexual harassment by news sources and co-workers is still a problem in the 1990s in spite of 30 year-old federal prohibitions, according to researchers at the University of Florida. In the University of Florida researchers' harassment survey, 60 per cent of the women said sexual harassment is at least somewhat a problem for women as reporters, photographers, editors and graphic artists and more than 1 in 10 (11.5%) said sexual harassment is a significant or very serious problem for women journalists. Lower percentage reported having substantial trouble with sexual harassment in their careers. Nonetheless, more than one third (36.1%) said sexual harassment had been at least somewhat a problem for them personally and 17 women (7.5%) reported having had significant or serious problems with sexual harassment during their careers (Walsh–Childers *et al.*, 1997).

Associated Press Managing Editors (APME) Association survey (Kossan, 1992) reported only 30 per cent of the respondents said their newspaper had clear guidelines for filing internal complaints about sexual harassment; while 95 per cent of the victims of sexual harassment are women. Moreover, 2 per cent of the men and 11 per cent of the women said sexual harassment or the fear of harassment affected their daily work habits; and half of those who said they had been sexually harassed said the harassment was in the form of annoying or degrading comments about sex.

Another study of women journalists in Washington, D.C. showed that 60 per cent of the women accredited to the Capitol Press Gallery had been sexually harassed. The researchers, McAdams and Beasley (1992), surveyed 273 women journalists and received responses from only 37 per cent of them. Of those who responded, 80 per cent said they believe sexual harassment is a problem for women journalist. McAdams and Beasley argue that the issue of sexual harassment among women journalists needs to be investigated and brought into the open so that individual women no longer have to deal with the problem alone. Studies show that sexual harassment has negative effects on women work performance as well as career advancement.

While the most prevalent form of harassment was annoying or degrading comments about sex, followed by offensive pictures or posters and annoying or degrading comments about women's bodies Flatow (1994) found that more than two-thirds of women working in the newsrooms of Indiana daily newspapers had indeed found them vulnerable to sexual harassment. In her survey of full time editorial employees working at 26 Indiana dailies, Flatow found that 22.4 per cent of the women and 6.6 per cent of the men had experienced physical sexual harassment at some point during their careers. The same percentage of men, but nearly three times the percentage of women (61.8%) reported experiencing verbal sexual harassment and nearly third of the women reported "nonverbal" sexual harassment.

Australia

In Australia, John Henningham (1996), surveyed 1068 new people in all mainstream news media. The total number of journalists employed by Australian mainstream news media is only about 4200. Australia, with about 250 journalists for every million people, has about half the proportion of journalists as the United States about 450 journalists for each million people. The study revealed that Australian journalists are young (median age 32), predominantly of Anglo-Saxon ethnic origin, and of middle class background. They are more likely to be male than female by a factor of two to one.

An assessment of the professional characteristics of Australian Journalists has concluded that in terms of traditional criteria (specialized knowledge, autonomy, organization, a code of ethics, and a service ideal), attainment of professional status is in progress but has not been realized (Henningham, 1990). The Australian survey found that almost two thirds of journalists would choose the word profession to describe their occupation. While this is a large majority, it remains problematic that a third of journalists do not favour the professional label.

Younger journalists, especially those aged under 35 were more likely to favour the professional label: of those over 50, most rejected the term. Possession of a university degree made little difference to concepts of journalism as a profession, but 74 per cent of journalism graduates saw themselves as members of a profession, compared with 62 per cent of arts graduates and 59 per cent of general communications graduates. Further, their ability at writing was the primary reason (often prompted by careers advisers at high school) while factors related to the glamour and excitement of journalist was second most important. The desire to serve the public was expressed by fewer than 4 per cent of journalists. Hence, a strongly service oriented notion of journalism was not found among Australian journalists.

China

A 1994 nation wide survey reports that 72 per cent of People's Republic of China (PRC) journalists was either satisfied or very satisfied with their job (Chen *et al.*, 1998). Other studies conducted in 1996 and 1997 show that when compared with their counterparts in Hong Kong and Taiwan, PRC journalists reported higher levels of overall job satisfaction.

Chan *et al.*, (2004) studied professional aspirations and job satisfaction of Chinese journalists. According to them, West Shanghai journalists derive satisfaction from job autonomy. However, those who prefer party media as ideal news outlet demonstrate higher levels of job satisfaction. For those embracing western professional media as ideals, job satisfaction is also positively associated with the journalist's emphasis on the interpretative role of the media, a belief rooted in Chinese party press ideology. Stronger positive valuation of professional media relative to that of the party media strengthens the positive relationship between job autonomy and job satisfaction. Implications of the findings are discussed in the understanding of media changes and journalistic professionalism in general.

Chan *et al.*, (2004) also examined tension between the "two masters" Chinese journalists serve: the communist's party and the public. They surveyed 515 Chinese journalists and concluded that job satisfaction was conditioned on the journalist perceptions about the system under which they operated. Though their findings were somewhat equivocal, job satisfaction tended to breed higher congruity between journalist's values and his or her perceptions of system values.

Russia

Most previous studies of Russian journalists have faced a common problem: the lack of access to the Soviet media system, although two studies of Soviet journalists and their work, published in the late 1970s and early 1980's still provide useful baseline data, some of which was synthesized by Remington (cited in Wei *et al.*, 1996). Studies conducted by researchers at Moscow State University in 1970-80 found an emphasis on the ideological and propaganda functions of the newspapers.

In a report of a research team's recent survey of Russian journalists found that Russian television remains the least innovative. The Soviet Union invented the pattern for broadcasting operations in communist countries: bloated, unimaginative bureaucracies devoted to singing the praise of the system (Mills, 1994).

In a study, Wei *et al.,* (1996) compared the perceptions of Russian and U.S. journalists regarding the importance of various professional roles. The findings were based on interviews with 1,156 U.S. journalists, which suggested that there are similarities between Russian and U.S. journalist's views but also some notable difference. According to the study, Russian wire service and U.S. radio journalists are the most conservative in their perceptions of the importance of various professional roles.

India

In India, Jeffrey (2000) estimated that there were 4700 journalists in early 1960's and around 13,000 in 1990's. In the year 1990's India had about 25,000 journalists on wages or retainers, which came up to one journalist for every 35,000 people. This excluded thousands of stringers and contributors. However, very few studies have been conducted to examine the sociological issues involved in the career of journalists in India. The first available empirical study on journalism education in India was the First Press Commission Report. According to the survey conducted for the commission in 1950, 201 out of a total 542 journalists i.e., 37 per cent had no university degree, 219 (40.4%) were graduates and 122 (22.5%) had a postgraduate degree. With respect to pre entry or in service training 460 out of the 542 journalists had no such training. Out of 82 journalists who received training, 25 were trained by newspapers themselves; 27 had taken a diploma in journalism and eight of them have a degree; the rest had gone through short courses in India or abroad. In India the journalists were mostly from middle or upper class with urban background. According to Second Press Commission (1984), Indian journalists particularly women came from middle or upper class families and were from urban background.

Eapen (1967) described the Indian Press as class media rather than mass media as it was owned, read and manned by urban middle class. He found that there was dissatisfaction in the professional areas of use of abilities and training, opportunity for originality and initiative and getting ahead in professional career. Malayalam journalists were professionally ahead of journalists from Bihar, Bombay and Madras. In the study, Eapen found that two-thirds of journalists were from forward caste; half of the reporters were in 23-34 age groups. Eapen's study showed that 90 per cent respondents were Hindus. The study revealed that 40 per cent of the respondents from Bihar, Maharashtra and Kerala were graduates and 31 per cent were postgraduates. The study also found that 34 per cent entered journalism for prestige, 27 per cent with service motto and 21 per cent for excitement.

A study of Delhi based journalists by Sharma (1990) revealed that over 60 per cent had postgraduate degree, 31 per cent entered journalism incidentally, 20 per cent attracted by the adventure and glamour while 38 per cent had other considerations like prestige, writing aptitude and parental occupation. Only 10 per cent opted for journalism to serve public. Sharma also studied that the extent of professionalism in terms of the observance of professional attributes like general systematic knowledge, norm of altruism, autonomy and monopoly. The researcher defined professionalism as structural characteristics or attributes of an occupation. Professionalism, he suggests, is a measurement of the attributes or characteristics of individuals in the occupation. The researcher states that the journalists have shown a low degree of altruism when the interests of the proprietors are adversely affected. They were ready to sacrifice public interests for self-interest and exploit their status and opportunities for non-journalistic purposes; sometimes they accept certain gratifications and inducement for publications or suppression of news.

A study of 200 women journalists revealed that gender continues to play an impending role in the lives of Indian women journalists both within the profession and in the wider society (Joseph, 1994). Verma and Narula (1998) in their study found that unlike the 1970s and 1980s, journalism in 1990s has become more of a career choice as salaries have gone up considerably. This is more so particularly after Government of India's 1991 budget, which gave boost to business journalism.

Agarwal (1995) examined the professional aspect of journalists in Jaipur to find out who enters journalism, their professional perceptions and the process of socialization. She used structured questionnaire interview and observation to gather data. In this study among the journalists working in Jaipur, men were predominant gender as only one in 8 was female. Agarwal's study revealed that nearly two thirds of Jaipur journalists were from urban areas and the remaining 10 per cent are from rural areas. A majority of journalists in Jaipur were in the age group of 26-30 years. In Jaipur, over 75 per cent were from open category, half of them were Brahmins, and Shudras (SC) constituted 17 per cent. Another significant aspect of the background was that most of the lower caste journalists were promoted from teleprinter operators and proofreaders or clerks. Agarwal suggested that the reasons for the high representation of journalists from the open category were due to the availability of modern education to that section of the society. One-third of journalists in Jaipur were postgraduates and 27 per cent had journalism education.

Inamdar (2003) in her study of "growth of online newspapers" found that majority of the online journalists were in the age group of 21-30 and most of the female respondents were between 21-31 years. She found that in Internet newspapers 7.6 per cent of the respondents had journalism education as against 72.3 per cent without journalism education. More female respondents had journalism education than their male counterparts. Further, she also found that as age increased, the number of male respondents also increased whereas the number of female respondents dropped. She studied growth of online newspapers in India and their implications on print media to find out the working conditions of online journalists and impact of online journalism on print media. With respect to the working conditions of online journalists the study concluded that there is awareness on the part of online journalists about the limitations of online journalism and they are being attracted towards the new media for better salaries and glamour. Inamdar found that there was a significant association between sex of respondents and their emoluments. Similarly Inamdar also found that as the age of the respondent increases the emoluments of the respondents also increased. In addition, the association between age and emoluments was significant.

In a comprehensive study across the country, Balasubramanya (2005) studied 835 journalists spread across 14 different states and working in newspapers and magazines of 11 languages. Only 20.12 per cent of them were women journalists and among them 38.68 per cent in the age group 20-30 years, 35.57 per cent in 31-40 age group, 17.37 per cent in 41-50, 6.71 per cent in 51-60, 1.68 per cent in 61-70 years group. A significant majority of 75 per cent was between 20-40 years. Regarding the marital status, 69.46 per cent were married, 29.2 per cent were unmarried, and 1.08 per cent divorced, 0.25 per cent widowed. Out of the total of 835, 41.7 per cent were postgraduates, 34.6 per cent were graduates, 7.43 per cent journalism graduates, 18.2 per cent postgraduates in journalism, 9.3 per cent have diploma or certificate courses in the journalism. Interestingly, the study noted that half of the journalists had freedom in the selection of a story while 2.5 per cent did not have freedom to select a story. As the age is increasing, one reaches the position of formulating policies of the newspaper or at least close to the policy-maker. By virtue of their position they get more freedom in their day-to-day operations.

The study has also noted that formal education in journalism is not compulsory to get into the profession. This is one of the reasons why journalism has not achieved the status of profession. Whereas the dynamic angle of the journalism education has been that more number of journalists have postgraduate qualification in journalism than the graduate degree in journalism which could be due to the fact that postgraduation in journalism is opened for all students from various disciplines without prior degree in journalism. According to him, majority of them have noble cause to join the profession like contribution something significant to the society as extremely important. The chance to help people was found as one important aspect of journalism and 53 per cent of the respondents subscribed to this view.

Sathi Reddy study (2005) found out that the median age of journalists in Andhra Pradesh is 33 years. The study also found out that satisfaction levels are related to professional issues like working/editing matters of significance and chance to be creative. However, the study also found out 4 per cent of the respondents expressed job satisfaction in relation to study. Further, the study examined the major complaint with the job which revealed that job insecurity was the major source of complaint.

A national workshop on women in journalism held in New Delhi in January 2002 also expressed that though the number of women in the media increased, their working conditions, especially in the small towns and in the regional language press, have actually deteriorated (Bhavani, and Vijaya Lakshmi, 2005). The workshop demanded for protection for all employment rights and benefits of women journalists and to implement Supreme Court directive on sexual harassment by media organizations. At the same time, women who are confident, hardworking, willing to take up the challenges reached top positions despite several hurdles in the profession. They have moved from coverage of soft news like fashions, art, beauty contests etc. to hard news such as politics, sports and war reporting. Although the proportion of women students in journalism education has increased, the number of students getting into media is not encouraging. The committee on the status of women in Indian journalism highlighted the low status of women in various spheres of women development (Press Institute of India Report, 2004).

The Press Institute of India report (2004) revealed that over two thirds of women journalists were below 34 years. The study found that many women journalists (even from established newspapers) work as daily wage labour, without an appointment letter, signing a muster roll at the end of the month to get Rs. 1,500-3000. Most women start working without appointment letters and are hired and fired on the whims of the management. Job insecurity was the highest in the regional language press because journalists are hired as daily wage earners. The study reported that major concerns were the contract system, the dilemma of childcare in conflict with profession, maternity leave and benefits and lack of transparency. The study reported that 3 per cent of respondents felt that being a mother was a disqualification for promotions. It also examined gender-based problems. About 23 per cent of respondents experienced sexual harassment and another 5 per cent was not sure about what constituted sexual harassment.

In north-eastern part of the country 40 per cent of the respondents have never been promoted. According to Kaul (2004) in the conflict-ridden northeastern part of the country, only 35 women work as print journalists in the seven states. Only 35 per cent of these are full-time employees; 40 per cent say they have never been promoted.

A study on women journalists in Andhra Pradesh showed that only half of the recruitments (43.3%) were made on permanent basis (Bhavani and Vijaya Lakshmi, 2005). In Telugu press 55.4 per cent and in the English press 60.9 per cent are working on permanent basis. 70 per cent of the sample is working in Telugu papers and 25 per cent in English newspapers. 91.7 per cent of those who are working in English newspapers have postgraduate degree whereas 55.6 per cent of the people who work with Telugu papers have post-graduate degree. 8.3 per cent English paper journalists are graduates and 38.9 per cent in Telugu papers are graduates.

Bhavani and Vijaya Lakshmi (2005) study revealed that majority of women journalists (77%) confined to desk were designated as chief sub-editors, desk in-charges, senior sub-editors, edition in-charge and sub-editors. It is interesting to note that 4.1 per cent of women in Telugu and 4 per cent in English press reached higher position and working as editors of the newspapers. The study found that only 18.9 per cent of respondents are working as reporters in Telugu papers and only 8 per cent are working in English newspapers.

In Andhra Pradesh, 35.1 per cent of women working in medium[2] newspapers are earning a salary of less than 2500 rupees per month. The percentage of women earning salary of Rs. 501-5000 per month is 35.1 per cent in medium newspapers and 29.8 per cent in large size newspapers. A higher percentage of 37.4 per cent women journalists in large newspapers are getting a salary of more than 500 rupees per month when compared with 2.8 per cent of women in medium size newspapers.

Job Satisfaction

Balasubramanya study (2005) observed that 51 per cent are satisfied to a great extent with their career as journalists and 41 per cent felt they were satisfied to some extent. 67 per cent of the respondents were proud of their profession as journalists.

Bhavani and Vijaya Lakshmi (2005) observed that 72 per cent of the women journalists have reported that they have no job satisfaction. 58 per cent of women journalists felt that their colleagues do not give proper encouragement and they are not given assignments of their interest (45%). The study noticed through personal interviews that women journalists are not happy with the work because no special incentives are given. Besides they do not receive appreciation for their work, and their views are not taken into consideration. Despite all these complaints, women journalists reported that they developed a sort of belongingness to the organization where they functioned.

Discrimination

Bhavani and Vijaya Lakshmi (2005) examined that 37 per cent felt that they are not given important work, 45 per cent claimed that they are denied the promotions, 46 per cent reported that the male colleagues find fault with their work and 53 per cent said that there is a difference in the payment of salaries when compared with male colleagues. That takes longer to get promotions is the opinion of 20 per cent of the respondents and 12 per cent claimed that they experienced discrimination sometimes. Coming to discrimination at work place only 36 per cent journalists said that they face discrimination at workplaces either always or sometimes and 36 per cent rarely and 28 per cent never experienced it.

Sexual Harassment

'Status of Women Journalists in India' report, commissioned by the National Commission for Women was prepared by the Press Institute of India (2004), is the first such attempt in the country to look at the problems of sexual harassment of journalists. According to the Press Institute of India study (2004), about 22 per cent of the 410 respondents said they had been sexually harassed at some point of time, but only 15 per cent made a formal complaint. A significant 40 per cent said they did not complain because the issue was not taken up seriously in their organization or that they were seen as over-reacting to a situation.

Facilities

In the study of Press Institute of India a small number (7%) of women working in newspapers said that the organization would provide crèche facility. Again a small percentage (7%) of women journalists claim that the organization provides free education to their children which is 9.1 per cent in big and 12.1 per cent in medium size organizations. Almost an equal percentage of women journalists have accreditation cards both in large (38.8%) and medium size (41.2%) newspapers. In the study, 2.6 per cent of respondents in large and 11.1 per cent in medium size newspapers reported that the management provides other facilities like canteen, separate cabin, insurance coverage (Press Institute of India Report, 2004).

Other Countries

In the United Kingdom, women join the field of journalism with a distinct difference in terms of their employment. Women have been underrepresented in the national dailies while they are overrepresented in commercial television and radio (Chambers *et al.*, 2004). The study also finds that 14 per cent of those women employed in newspapers become deputy editors while 20 per cent of men reach the same rank. In periodicals and broadcasting the difference was more pronounced with 27 per cent of women becoming editors or deputy editors compared to 40 per cent of men and 12 per cent of women became section editors or heads compared to 16 per cent of men.

Canada's news media workforce is dominated by young, highly educated males. Women news workers are younger than their male counterparts and have more education (especially professional training), have less work experience (Pollard, 1995). In Canada overall mean age of news workers is 34.9 years. Newspaper workers are older than those in broadcasting and more likely to be married and be Anglophones. Among women 31.9 per cent are married and their mean age is 30.4 years. Among the women 57 per cent are single and others are 11.1 per cent.

Among the Netherlands journalists, most of them were men aged between 30 and 40 years (Dueze, 2003). In Uganda, the median age of Ugandan journalists was 31 years and a majority of them were men (Mwesige, 2004). In Tanzania, Ramprasad (2001) study found that management had strong influence on reporting practices. It is followed by government position and personal level influence respectively.

END NOTES

1. In 1993, the Supreme Court of India defined sexual harassment as an activity which includes such unwelcome sexually determined behaviour (whether directly or by implication) as:
   - *(a)* physical contact and advances;
   - *(b)* a demand or request for sexual favours;
   - *(c)* sexually coloured remarks;

(*d*) showing pornography;

(*e*) any other unwelcome physical, verbal or non-verbal conduct of sexual nature.

Where any of these acts is committed in circumstances where under the victim of such conduct has a reasonable apprehension that in relation to the victim's employment or work whether she is drawing salary, or honorarium or voluntary, whether in government, public or private enterprise such conduct can be humiliating and may constitute a health and safety problem. It is discriminatory for instances when the woman has reasonable grounds to believe that her objection would disadvantage her in connection with her employment or work including recruiting or promotion or when it creates a hostile work environment. Adverse consequences might be visited if the victim does not consent to the conduct in question or raises any objection thereto (Ref..)

2. Newspapers are classified as big, medium, and small in terms of their circulation. Generally newspapers having above one lakh circulation are called large newspapers, those which have circulation between 50,000 and one lakh, are classified as medium size newspapers and below 50,000 are counted as small size newspapers.

2

RESEARCH METHODOLOGY

With the growth of the new communication technologies such as cable television, computers, the Internet, satellites and telecommunications information dissemination has been increasingly influencing the Indian society (Singhal and Rogers, 2001: 19). Consequently, the mass communication channels in India have been expanding. With the availability of new technology, newspaper publication has increased manifold and India publishes more daily newspapers than any other country in Asia, covering a range of languages and cultural diversity that is unparalleled in the world (Singhal and Rogers: 2001: 54).

By the turn of 2006, there were over 55,000 newspapers and periodicals published in 93 languages. In respect of radio broadcasting, there were only 6 stations of All India Radio (AIR) located in metropolitan cities in India at the time of Independence (Kohli, 2006). AIR has 110 primary channels, 30 Vividh Bharthi stations, 75 local radio stations and four FM channels (Kohli, 2006). The FM radio has grown in the country with over 40 stations. By 2006, broadcasts of All India Radio programmes were heard in 110 million households in 24 languages and 146 dialects. Further, television too has grown immensely. About 50 per cent of India's population regularly watches television networks like Zee TV, STAR TV, SONY, CNN, BBC and many others which are broadcasting various programmes.

In particular, the federal state of Andhra Pradesh has witnessed a media boom. Newspapers with chain editions,

FM radio stations and new television networks continuously supply news and entertainment programmes. For example, *Eenadu,* the largest circulated daily has 23 chain editions. The television networks such as *Etv2, Gemini* and *TV9* telecast 24-hour news. Because of proliferation of mass communication channels, the employment of women in various mass media channels is growing. With this background, the present study is taken up to examine the sociological issues involved in the lives of women media workers. Therefore the present study makes an attempt to ascertain answers to the following research questions.

Research Questions

Research questions pertinent to the study are:

1. Is the employment affecting the women in relation to their personal life?
2. If so, how do working women in media cope with the family life?
3. How do these media women with children make arrangements for childcare?
4. Are these women satisfied with their employment?
5. In an increasingly male dominated workplace setting, are these women facing any problems?
6. Over all, how do these media women assess the professional satisfaction?

Objectives of the Study

In view of these research questions, the present study has the following objectives:

1. To find out the socio-demographic profile of the working media women in the study sample;
2. To find out the family details such as spouse employment, education, income and so on, which impact the working media women's married life;

3. To examine the satisfaction levels of working media women in the sample in relation to childcare arrangements;
4. To examine the work setting *vis-a-vis* professional freedom of the working media women in the study sample, and
5. To ascertain the professional satisfaction of working media women in the study sample in different media organizations.

Research Setting

The research setting of the study is the state of Andhra Pradesh in which three cities viz., Hyderabad, Vijayawada and Visakhapatnam have been the focus of the study. Many newspaper publications such as *Eenadu, Andhra Bhoomi, Vaartha, Deccan Chronicle, The Hindu,* along with *All India Radio* AM and FM stations and the headquarters of TV networks are located in these three cities. Hyderabad, the capital city of the state has the highest number of newspaper publications, TV network headquarters, *All India Radio* station and FM station. Next, Vijayawada too has the chain editions of *Eenadu, Andhra Jyothi, Andhra Bhoomi, Vaartha, The Hindu, New Indian Express, Deccan Chronicle* and so on. An *AIR* station is located here. Similarly, Visakhapatnam is the fastest growing industrial city with many newspaper publication centers like *The Hindu, New Indian Express, Deccan Chronicle, Eenadu, Andhra Jyothi, Andhra Bhoomi* and *Vaartha,* while *AIR* station and *Vividh Bharthi* stations are located here. A private FM station, *SFM* is also operating from here. Apart from big publications, small newspapers like *Visakha Samacharam* are also being published from the city.

Study Sample

In view of the objectives, the researchers proposed to use a survey method while adopting a purposive sampling method to collect data pertaining to the study. Since the study focuses on working media women, the researcher in a preliminary survey listed out the total number of media women working in three mass communication channels i.e. newspapers, TV networks and radio network that come under the study across the state. It has been found out that a total of 145 women are working in the following organizations (Table 3).

Once the total number of women working in three cities in different media organizations was available, the researchers, keeping in view the objectives of the study, decided to administer a questionnaire. The researchers approached the respondents with a request to fill the questionnaire. However, a total of 127 respondents accepted to fill the questionnaire while 18 rejected the request (See Table 4).

Table-3
Media Organization Where Media Women are Working

Media Organization	*Number of Women Working*	
	Accepted to Fill the Questionnaire	*Refused to Fill the Questionnaire*
Newspaper		
Andhra Bhoomi	2	-
Andhra Jyothi	8	-
Deccan Chronicle	3	3
Economic Times	3	-
Eenadu	11	3
New Indian Express	4	-
Prajasakhti	8	-
The Hindu	15	4
Times of India	8	-
Vaartha	8	4
Visakha Samacharam	1	-

Contd...

Media Organization	*Number of Women Working*	
	Accepted to Fill the Questionnaire	*Refused to Fill the Questionnaire*
Visalandhra	6	-
Television Channel		
Etv	18	4
Etv2	7	-
TV9	14	-
Excel	1	-
Radio		
All India Radio	10	-
Total	**127**	**18**

Table–4
Distribution of Respondents in Three Cities by their Organization

Media Organization	*Hyderabad*	*Visakhapatnam*	*Vijayawada*
	f	*f*	*f*
Newspaper			
Andhra Bhoomi	2	-	-
Andhra Jyothi	8	-	-
Deccan Chronicle	3	-	-
Economic Times	3	-	-
Eenadu	9	-	2
New Indian Express	3	1	-
Prajasakhti	6	1	1
The Hindu	11	3	1
Times of India	7	1	-

Contd...

Media Organization	*Hyderabad*	*Visakhapatnam*	*Vijayawada*
	f	*f*	*f*
Vaartha	7	1	-
Visakha Samacharam	-	1	-
Visalandhra	1	-	5
Television Channel			
Etv	18	-	-
Etv2	7	-	-
TV9	14	-	-
Excel	-	1	-
Radio			
All India Radio	1	9	-
Total	**100**	**18**	**9**

N = 127

Operational Definition

Working Media Women

The operational definition of working media women in the present study is described as women who work in media organizations as reporters, editors, script writers, producers and anchors of different TV channels and radio jockeys.

Data Collection Instrument

The data collection instrument was a structured questionnaire consisting of close-ended and open-ended questions. The structured questionnaire was divided into six parts. Part I consisted of questions related to identification data of the respondents such as caste, religion, marital status, mother tongue and so on. Part II had questions dealing with the family, family size, spouse details etc. Part III comprised questions relating to marriage and children. The questions in this section specifically were designed to ascertain information about type of marriage, reasons for untimely marriage, pregnancy, childcare arrangements, recreation etc. Part IV dealt with work setting. These questions in this section focused on type of appointment, motivation for joining the present job, type of duty, work timing and so on. Specifically Part V has questions in relation to work environment in the organization such as treatment from male colleagues, type of problems in the office etc. Further, the last section focused on job satisfaction and career (See Appendix I).

Pilot Study

The questionnaire thus prepared was pilot tested in Visakhapatnam and Hyderabad cities. Initially, 20 media women were administered the questionnaire. After the pilot study, some questions on childcare arrangements and family details required modifications, the researcher incorporated such changes in the questionnaire.

Data Collection Procedure

The process of data collection took three months i.e., November, December 2006 and January 2007. As the researchers were former journalists, who worked in newspapers, they approached the respondents with a questionnaire. Further, they explained the purpose of the study to the identified respondents who cooperated with them in filling the questionnaires. As media women were working in shifts, they asked the researchers to leave the questionnaire with them. In spite of being given the questionnaire, they did not return it in time. In Hyderabad city, it took more than one month for the researcher to collect data pertaining to the study.

Problems in Data Collection

In the process of data collection, the researchers faced a few problems such as frequent travels, staying in Vijayawada, and Hyderabad for the purpose of meeting the respondents and persuading some of the respondents to return the filled-in questionnaires.

As the researchers were living in Visakhapatnam, they had to travel to Vijayawada and Hyderabad in the weekends to meet some respondents. Although prior appointments were fixed with few respondents, they were not available on account of special assignments. In some occasions, the respondents were given irregular weekly offs with sudden developments that were arising in the newspaper offices. Another problem was in meeting some respondents working in television stations. Some respondents expressed the view that they wanted to meet the researchers only in their offices and while some others invited her to their house. Because of these problems, the researchers stayed in Hyderabad to collect the data. Further, a specific problem arose with 7 journalists working in two English dailies, who refused to fill the questionnaire once they had read them. They pointed out that they did not like to disclose the information, asked in the questionnaire.

Data Reduction and Analysis

The data thus collected were tabulated and analyzed by using SPSS. The analysis was done to examine the relationship between variables. Percentages were calculated and appropriate statistical tests were applied wherever necessary.

The study, however, has limitations, as the results cannot be generalized to all the working media women. Since the sampling method adopted for the study is purposive, the results are confined to the respondents only in the sample. Further, the study has been taken up in three cities in the state; the results reflect the issues related to working media women in these cities, while excluding the working media women from other small towns in the state.

3

PROFILE OF WORKING MEDIA WOMEN

The objective of the present chapter is to provide the profile of the respondents such as age, education, income and so on.

Characteristics

A total of 127 respondents came up for final analysis. Out of these 127, 78.7 per cent respondents were from Hyderabad while 14.2 per cent were from Visakhapatnam and remaining 7.1 per cent were from Vijayawada. In these 127 respondents, 88 (69.3%) were from print media while 39 (30.7%) were from electronic media such as radio and television networks. However, 69.3 per cent respondents who represented print media belonged to 12 newspapers, while 30.7 per cent journalists who represented electronic media belonged to 4 TV channels and one radio network, i.e., government controlled All India Radio (See Table 5 and 6).

Table-5

Total Number of Respondents from Three Cities

Place	*f*	%
Hyderabad	100	78.7
Visakhapatnam	18	14.2
Vijayawada	9	7.1
Total	**127**	**100**

Table-6
Total Number of Respondents from Media Organizations

Media Organization	*f*	%
Newspapers	88	69.3
Radio and TV channels	39	30.7
Total	**127**	**100**

N = 127

Out of 88 print media journalists, majority (11.8%) of the respondents were from one English newspaper, *The Hindu* followed by Telugu daily *Eenadu* (8.7%). Four other dailies namely viz., *Andhra Jyothi, Prajasakhti, Times of India* and *Vaartha* were in the next place. In respect of television networks, *Etv* (14.1%) had more percentage of respondents followed by *TV9* (11.0%), *Etv2* (5.5%) and *Excel Media* (0.8%). With regard to radio, all the respondents belonged to *All India Radio* (See Table 7).

Table-7
Percentage Distribution of Respondents by Media Organization

Media Organization	*f*	%
Newspaper		
Andhra Bhoomi	2	1.6
Andhra Jyothi	8	6.3
Deccan Chronicle	3	2.4
Economic Times	3	2.4
Eenadu	11	8.7
New Indian Express	4	3.1
Prajasakhti	8	6.3
The Hindu	15	11.8
Times of India	8	6.3
Vaartha	8	6.3

Contd...

Media Organization	*f*	%
Visakha Samacharam	1	0.8
Visalandhra	6	4.7
Television Channel		
Etv	18	14.1
Etv2	7	5.5
Excel	1	0.8
TV9	14	11.0
Radio		
All India Radio	10	7.9
Total	**127**	**100**

Designation

In the study, it was found that the respondents were representing varied jobs in the mass media and yet broadly they belonged to reporting, editing, script writing, producing and anchoring of the programmes. Though the nature of the job apparently was the same; their designations varied depending upon the organization they were working for. Therefore, the distribution of respondents by their designation showed that nearly 30 per cent of them were working as sub-editors and 18.9 per cent were reporters in the print media. About 17 per cent were copy editors who were working for various television channels. In the senior media women category, 6.2 per cent were senior sub-editors. Next place were occupied by radio jockeys (3.9%) of FM Radio in All India Radio. Chief sub-editors and reporters/sub-editors were 3.1 per cent each and senior reporters and principle correspondents were 2.4 per cent. Proof-readers and transmission executives were 1.6 per cent each. Remaining categories like Bureau Chief, News Editor, Programme Associate, Station Director, Script Writer, Photographer, Senior Announcer, Senior Feature Writer, Feature Editor, Copy Editor/News Reader, Radio Producer were 0.8 per cent each (See Table 8). Overall, 8.7 per cent of the sample respondents occupy elevated positions and are in a decision making position.

Table–8
Distribution of Respondents by Designation

Designation	*f*	%
Bureau Chief	1	0.8
Chief Sub-Editor	4	3.1
Copy Editor	22	17.3
Copy Editor/News Reader	1	0.8
Features Editor	1	0.8
News Editor	1	0.8
Photographer	1	0.8
Principle Correspondent	3	2.4
Programme Associate	1	0.8
Proof-reader	2	1.6
Radio Jockey	5	3.9
Radio Producer	1	0.8
Reporter	24	18.9
Reporter/Copy Editor	1	0.8
Reporter/Sub-Editor	4	3.1
Script Writer	1	0.8
Senior Announcer	1	0.8
Senior Feature Writer	1	0.8
Senior Reporter	3	2.4
Senior Sub-Editor	8	6.2
Station Director	1	0.8
Sub-Editor	38	29.9
Transmission Executive	2	1.6
Total	**127**	**100**

Caste

In Indian society, caste hierarchy plays a predominant role and every individual belongs to one caste or another. These castes for the purpose of government records are divided into three: Open category, backward category and scheduled category or caste. Open category represents the upper castes in social hierarchy. Table 9 shows the caste distribution of the total 127 respondents. 89 per cent of them belong to open category, 10.2 per cent are from backward class category and only 0.8 per cent belong to scheduled caste (Table 9). Media women who belong to backward caste are found working in all types of media organizations. Two women each who belong to backward caste are working in *Etv, Eenadu* and *All India Radio.* One each are found in *Etv2, Excel, New Indian Express, Times of India, TV9, Vaartha, Visaalandhra.* The lone scheduled caste woman is with *Visaalandhra* (Table 10).

Table-9
Distribution of Respondents by Caste

Caste	*f*	%
O.C.	113	89.0
B.C.	13	10.2
S.C.	1	0.8
Total	**127**	**100**

N = 127

Table-10
Caste-wise Distribution of Respondents by Media Organizations

Media Organization	*OC*		*BC*		*SC*	
	f	%	*f*	%	*f*	%
Newspaper						
Andhra Bhoomi	2	1.8	-	-	-	-
Andhra Jyothi	8	7.1	-	-	-	-

Contd...

Media Organization	*OC*		*BC*		*SC*	
	f	%	*f*	%	*f*	%
Deccan Chronicle	3	2.7	-	-	-	-
Economic Times	3	2.7	-	-	-	-
Eenadu	10	8.8	1	7.7	-	-
New Indian Express	3	2.7	1	7.7	-	-
Prajasakhti	8	7.1	-	-	-	-
The Hindu	15	13.3	-	-	-	-
Times of India	7	6.2	1	7.7	-	-
Vaartha	7	6.2	1	7.7	-	—
Visakha Samacharam	1	0.9	-	-	-	-
Visalandhra	4	3.5	1	7.7	1	100
Television Channel						
Etv	15	13.2	3	23.0	-	-
Etv2	6	5.3	1	7.7	-	-
TV9	12	10.6	2	15.4	-	-
Excel	-	-	1	7.7	-	-
Radio						
All India Radio	9	7.9	1	7.7	-	-
Total	**113**	**100**	**13**	**100**	**1**	**100**

N = 127

Age

Age distribution of respondent's shows that more than half of them (54.4%) are in the age group of 21-30 years, while 31.5 per cent are in the group of 31-40 years, 10.2 per cent are in 41-50 and 3.9 per cent in 51-60 years group. The minimum and maximum ages of the respondents are 21 and 59 years respectively. The mean age of the respondents has come to

31.29 years. The median age of the respondent is 28 years (Table 12). One interesting finding is the respondents working in TV channels are below 40 years, while majority of them are in the age group of 21-30 (Table 11 and Figure 1).

Table-11
Distribution of Respondents by Age from Media Organizations

Media Organization	*21-30*		*31-40*		*41-50*		*51-60*	
	f	%	*f*	%	*f*	%	*f*	%
Newspaper								
Andhra Bhoomi	-	-	2	5.0	-	-	-	-
Andhra Jyothi	-	-	4	10.0	3	23.0	1	20.0
Deccan Chronicle	2	2.9	-	-	1	7.7	-	-
Economic Times	3	4.3	-	-	-	-	-	-
Eenadu	5	7.3	4	10.0	2	15.4	-	-
New Indian Express	3	4.3	1	2.5	-	-	-	-
Prajasakhti	5	7.3	1	2.5	2	15.4	-	-
The Hindu	6	8.7	7	17.5	2	15.4	-	-
Times of India	8	11.6	-	-	-	-	-	-
Vaartha	-	-	6	15.0	2	15.4	-	-
Visakha Samacharam	-	-	-	-	-	-	1	20.0
Visalandhra	1	1.4	4	10.0	1	7.7	-	-
Television Channel								
Etv	17	24.6	1	2.5	-	-	-	-
Etv2	6	8.7	1	2.5	-	-	-	-
Excel	-	-	1	2.5	-	-	-	-
TV9	11	16.0	3	7.5	-	-	-	-
Radio								
All India Radio	2	2.9	5	12.5	-	-	3	60.0
Total	**69**	**100**	**40**	**100**	**13**	**100**	**5**	**100**

N = 127

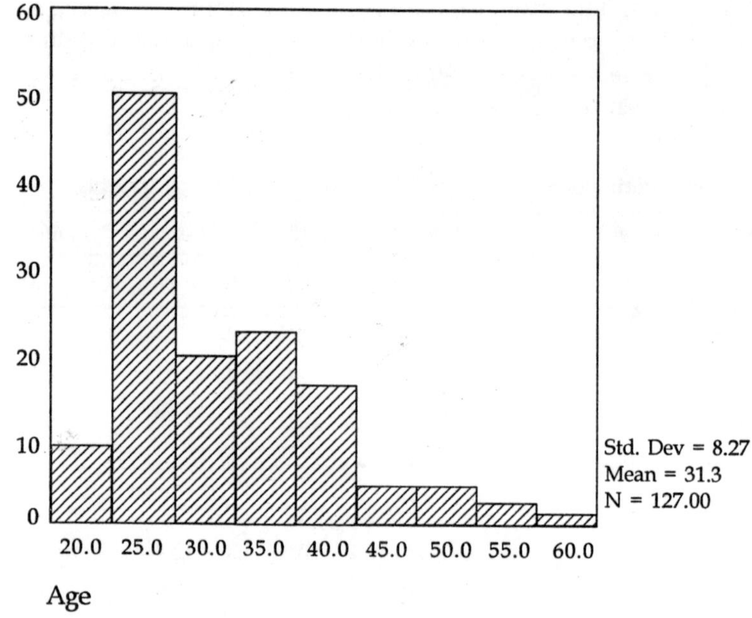

Figure 1: Shows the Age Distribution of Respondents

Table–12
Stem and Leaf Display[1] of Age of the Respondents

5	22459
4	01122222446689
3	000111222222 33334444444 556666677778888899 9
2	1112222222333333333333444444555555556666666666666666 7777778888899

N = 127

Note: See Appendix II.
Stem: 10, Leaf: Integer.

Religion

In the total sample of 127, 90.6 per cent of the respondents belong to Hindu religion (Table 13), followed by Muslims (5.5%) and Christians (3.9%). Among the Muslims two each from *Etv* and *Times of India,* one respondent each is from *Deccan Chronicle* and *New Indian Express.* Among the Christians two are from *The Hindu,* one each from *Etv, Vaartha* and *Deccan Chronicle.*

Table-13
Distribution of Respondents by Religion

Religion	*f*	%
Hindu	115	90.6
Muslim	7	5.5
Christian	5	3.9
Total	**127**	**100**

Marital Status

With regard to the marital status more than half of them (62.2%) are married, while 36.2 per cent are unmarried and two of them i.e., 1.6 per cent are widows (See Table 14).

Table-14
Distribution of Respondents by Marital Status

Marital Status	*f*	%
Married	79	62.2
Unmarried	46	36.2
Widow	2	1.6
Total	**127**	**100**

Level of Education

The level of education of the respondents is seen in Table 15. 65.4 per cent are postgraduates followed by 30.7 per cent graduates and 3.9 per cent are undergraduates.

Specifically more (64.6%) than half of the respondents did a course in journalism. Among them 54.9 per cent hold a postgraduate degree in Journalism, 39 per cent have diplomas and 6.1 per cent completed a certificate course in Journalism.

Table-15
Distribution of Respondents by Level of Education

Level of Education	*f*	%
Postgraduate	83	65.4
Graduate	39	30.7
Under Graduate	5	3.9
Total	**127**	**100**

Income

Among the 127 respondents, 51.2 per cent get less than one lakh of rupees per annum, while 15.8 per cent are in the income range of Rs. 1.01-1.50 lakhs. 13.4 per cent are in the income group of Rs. 1.51-2.00 lakhs followed by 10.2 per cent each in Rs. 2.01–2.50 lakhs. Media women who are drawing more than Rs. 2.50 lakhs per annum are few in number. 4.7 per cent have income in the range of Rs. 2.51-3.00 lakhs and another 4.7 per cent get above 3 lakhs of rupees. The mean income of the respondents is Rs. 62,000 per annum (Table 16 and Table 17).

Table-16
Distribution of Respondents by Income

Income (in Lakhs)	*f*	%
0-0.50	13	10.2
0.51-1.00	52	41.0
1.01-1.50	20	15.8
1.51-2.00	17	13.4
2.01-2.50	13	10.2
2.51-3.00	6	4.7
3.00 +	6	4.7
Total	**127**	**100**

Table-17
Percentage Distribution of Respondents from Different Income[a] Groups in Media Organizations

Media Organization	*0-50*		*51-1.00*		*1.01-1.50*		*1.51-2.00*		*2.01-2.50*		*2.51-3.00*		*Above 3 Lakhs*	
	f	%	*f*	%	*f*	%	*f*	%	*f*	%	*f*	%	*f*	%
Newspaper														
Andhra Bhoomi	-	-	2	3.9	-	-	-	-	-	-	-	-	-	-
Andhra Jyothi	1	7.7	7	13.5	-	-	-	-	-	-	-	-	-	-
Deccan Chronicle	-	-	-	-	1	5.0	1	5.9	1	7.7	-	-	-	-
Economic Times	-	-	-	-	-	-	-	-	1	7.7	1	16.7	1	16.7
Eenadu	-	-	3	5.8	4	20.0	3	17.6	1	7.7	-	-	-	-
New Indian Express	-	-	1	1.9	-	-	2	11.8	-	-	1	16.7	-	-
Prajasa-khti	2	15.5	4	7.7	1	5.0	1	5.9	-	-	-	-	-	-
The India	-	-	-	-	3	15.0	4	23.5	4	30.7	2	33.3	2	33.3
Times of India	-	-	1	1.9	2	10.0	1	5.9	3	23.1	-	-	1	16.7
Vaartha	1	7.7	6	11.5	1	5.0	-	-	-	-	-	-	-	-
Visakha Samacharam	-	-	-	-	1	5.0	-	-	-	-	-	-	-	-
Visal-andhra	3	23.0	3	5.8	-	-	-	-	-	-	-	-	-	-

Contd...

Media Organization	*0-50*		*51-1.00*		*1.01-1.50*		*1.51-2.00*		*2.01-2.50*		*2.51-3.00*		*Above 3 Lakhs*	
	f	*%*	*f*	*%*	*f*	*%*	*f*	*%*	*f*	*%*	*f*	*%*	*f*	*%*
Television Channel														
Etv	1	7.7	15	28.8	2	10.0	-	-	-	-	-	-	-	-
Etv2	1	7.7	5	9.6	1	5.0	-	-	-	-	-	-	-	-
Excel	-	-	1	1.9	-	-	-	-	-	-	-	-	-	-
TV9	1	7.7	3	5.8	4	20.0	5	29.4	-	-	1	16.7	-	-
Radio														
All India Radio	3	23.0	1	1.9	-	-	-	-	3	23.1	1	16.7	2	33.3
Total	**13**	**100**	**52**	**100**	**20**	**100**	**17**	**100**	**13**	**100**	**6**	**100**	**6**	**100**

a = income is given in rupees.

Mother Tongue

In order to ascertain how many of the respondents speak Telugu as their mother tongue, the researcher asked a question about the mother tongue of the respondent. The mother tongue of nearly two thirds of the respondent's is Telugu, followed by Hindi (7.9%), Malayalam (5.5%), Bengali (5.5%). The next places are occupied by Tamil (4.7%), Urdu (4.7%), Gujarati (2.4%), Kannada (1.6%) and Assamese, Oriya, Rajasthani, Sindhi with 0.8 per cent each (Table 18).

In terms of the media organizations they are working in, 59.6 per cent respondents from electronic media speak Telugu followed by Hindi (11.5%), Bengali (9.6%), Urdu (7.8%), Gujarati (5.8%), Kannada, Oriya, Sindhi (1.9%) each. In print media Telugu people are more (68%) in number followed by Malayalam (9.3%), Tamil (8.0%), Hindi (5.3%), Urdu and Bengali (2.6%); and Rajasthani, Kannada, Assamese 1.4 per cent each. It is obvious that those respondents who speak other

Table-18
Distribution of Respondents by Mother Tongue

Mother Tongue	*f*	%
Telugu	82	64.5
Hindi	10	7.9
Malayalam	7	5.5
Bengali	7	5.5
Tamil	6	4.7
Urdu	6	4.7
Gujarati	3	2.4
Kannada	2	1.6
Assamese	1	0.8
Oriya	1	0.8
Rajasthani	1	0.8
Sindhi	1	0.8
Total	**127**	**100**

languages are working in English newspapers and other language channels (Table 19).

Table-19
Distribution of Respondents by Mother Tongue in Relation to Different Media

Mother Tongue	*Media Organization*	
	Electronic (n = 52)	*Print (n = 75)*
Assamese	-	1.4
Bengali	9.6	2.6
Gujarati	5.8	-
Hindi	11.5	5.3

Contd...

Mother Tongue	Media Organization	
	Electronic (n = 52)	Print (n = 75)
Kannada	1.9	1.4
Malayalam	-	9.3
Oriya	1.9	-
Rajasthani	-	1.4
Sindhi	1.9	-
Tamil	-	8.0
Telugu	59.6	68.0
Urdu	7.8	2.6
Total	**100.0**	**100.0**

N = 127

Native Place

Majority (80.3%) of the respondents in the study belong to Hyderabad while 12.6 per cent are from Visakhapatnam and 7.1 per cent are from Vijayawada as their native place (Table 20). Most (78.7%) of the respondents have migrated to their present place of working. The rest of 21.3 per cent are working in their native places.

Table-20
Distribution of Respondents by their Native Place

Native Place	f	%
Hyderabad	102	80.3
Visakhapatnam	16	12.6
Vijayawada	9	7.1
Total	**127**	**100**

The reasons for the migration of the media women are also highly varied. Two thirds of the respondents have migrated to their present place of working because of employment, while 10 per cent have migrated after their marriage and 9 per cent of them had to move away from the native places because of father's job (See Table 21).

Table-21
Reason Reported by Respondents for Migration

Reason for Migration	*f*	%
Father's job	9	9
Fathers transfer	2	2
Fathers business	1	1
Self job	65	65
Husband's job	7	7
Job	1	1
Children's education	1	1
After marriage	10	10
Studies	1	1
Transfer	2	2
Cannot say	1	1
Total	**100**	**100**

Property

In the total sample of 127, 63.8 per cent of the respondents do not own any property whereas, 36.2 per cent have property. The distribution of the type of property (Table 22) owned by respondent's shows that 36.5 per cent have own houses followed by 31.7 per cent own apartments and 30.2 per cent own land. Some of the respondents own more than one type of property. Other than house, apartment and land, a few respondents have reported that they own property such as shops, business premises etc.

Table-22
Type of Property Owned by Respondents

Property	*f*	%
House	23	36.5
Apartment	20	31.7
Land	19	30.2
Business premises	1	1.6
Total	**63**	**100**

Family

An attempt was made to ascertain the type of the family of the respondent in the present study. Family is the primary institution where the parents, children, uncles, aunts, grandparents stay together and the socialization process of the young takes place here. This is one of the cultural institutions to reinforce values to the young and provide guidelines in terms of norms and values. There are three types of families. Joint family is defined as a union of members related to both the partners in the couple and either of the partners, their children, their siblings, daughters-in-law, grandchildren who stay under a common roof and have common dining and cooking. The hold on income and property rests with the head of the family who is the elder of the family.

A nuclear family is defined as a family with a bond of parents and children staying separately from their parents and other relatives but have the share of the common property. The extended family is a family where the parents, children and some distant family relatives stay with them temporarily for some time. In the study, above 84.2 per cent of the respondents reported that theirs is a nuclear family while 15 per cent reported that they hail from joint family. However 0.8 per cent of the respondents reported extended family (Table 23).

Table-23
Distribution of Respondents by Type of Family

Type of Family	*f*	%
Nuclear	107	84.2
Joint Family	19	15.0
Extended Family	1	0.8
Total	**127**	**100**

4

WORKING MEDIA WOMEN: MARRIAGE, SPOUSE AND CHILDREN

In this chapter details about respondent's marriage, spouse, children, and childcare arrangements, followed by job-related information are presented.

Spouse's Details

In the following pages details about respondent's spouse are presented from Table 24 to 27. As regards the age of the respondent's spouse, one fourth of them were in the age group of 41–45 followed by 21.6 per cent in the age group of 31-35, and 20.3 per cent in 36-40 years group. About 16 per cent of the respondent's spouses are found to be in 25-30 years age group (Table 24). The minimum and maximum ages of the respondent's spouses are 26 and 63 years. The mean age of the respondent's spouse has come to 38.5 years.

Table–24

Age Distribution of Respondent's Spouse

Age Group	*% (n=74)*
25-30	16.2
31-35	21.6
36-40	20.3
41-45	28.4

Contd...

Age Group	*% (n=74)*
46-50	5.4
51-55	5.4
56-60	2.7
Total	**100**

In respect of the level of education of the respondent's spouse about 57 per cent are graduates and 36.5 per cent are postgraduates. 5.4 per cent hold diplomas and negligible number of them are undergraduates (Table 25).

Table-25
Level of Education of Respondent's Spouse

Level of Education	*% (n=74)*
Diploma	5.4
Under Graduate	1.3
Graduate	56.8
Postgraduate	36.5
Total	**100**

When it comes to the income of the respondent's spouse 24.3 per cent reported that their husband's income is in the range of Rs. 1.01-1.50 lakhs per annum followed by 12.2 per cent who reported that their spouse's income is between Rs. 2.51 lakhs and 3.00 lakhs. Nearly 11 per cent said that their spouse's income is above 4 lakhs of rupees per annum. Since one respondent's spouse retired from the service, his income was reported to be less than one lakh. Another respondent's spouse is a non-resident Indian working in the USA earning almost Rs. 50 lakhs per annum (Table 26).

Respondents reported the details of the spouse's employment and half of them are working in private firms. 13.5 per cent are in Government Service; while 12.1 per cent are journalists and 6.8 per cent are self-employed (Table 27). Mostly, the respondent's spouse is working in private firms as clerks, managers, skilled workers and so on. These people earn on an average Rs. 8,000 per month.

Table-26
Annual Income Distribution of Respondent's Spouse

Income (Lakhs)	*% (n=73)*
Upto 0.50	8.1
0.51-1.00	20.3
1.01-1.50	24.3
1.51-2.00	13.5
2.01-2.50	5.4
2.51-3.00	12.2
3.01-3.50	4.1
3.51- 4.00	1.3
Above 4 lakhs	10.8
Total	**100**

Table-27
Employment Details of Respondent's Spouse

Spouse's Employment	*% (n=74)*
Private Company	55.4
Government Service	13.5
Journalists	12.1
Business	9.4
Bank Officers	2.7
Pharmacist	1.4
Software Engineer	1.4
Social Worker	1.4
Retired Lecturer	1.4
Advocate	1.4
Total	**100**

Marriage

Out of 127 respondents 81 respondents are married while 46 are unmarried. Among the 81 respondents who are married, 72.8 per cent had arranged marriages and 23.5 per cent of them reported love marriages (Table 28). The rest (3.7%) of them had some other type of marriage.

Table-28
Type of Marriage of the Respondent

Type of Marriage	*f*	%
Arranged	59	72.8
Love	19	23.5
Any other	3	3.7
Total	**81**	**100**

Among the married, 59.3 per cent got married when they were in the age group of 21-25 years followed by 24.7 per cent in the 26–30 years group. 12.3 per cent got married before attaining the age of 20 (Table 29). About 4 per cent of the respondents in the sample got married after 30 years of age. The minimum and maximum ages of marriages are 16 and 36 years. The mean age of the respondent's marriage was 24.6 years.

Table-29
Age of Marriage of the Respondent

Age of Marriage (Years)	*f*	%
Below 20	10	12.3
21-25	48	59.3
26-30	20	24.7
31-35	2	2.5
Above 35	1	1.2
Total	**81**	**100**

When asked about the time of their marriage, majority (77.8%) of them reported that they got married in time (Table 30). Of the 81 respondents 17.3 per cent reported that they had delayed marriage and 5 per cent got married early.

Table-30
Time of Marriage of the Respondent

Time of Marriage	*f*	%
Timely	63	77.8
Delayed	14	17.3
Early	4	4.9
Total	**81**	**100**

In response to the reasons for early marriages, 50.0 per cent said that they did not know the specific reason, while 25 per cent reported that it was a family affair, and one respondent said that it was the right age according to the family tradition (Table 31).

Table-31
Reason for Early Marriage

Reason for Early Marriage	*f*	%
Family affair	1	25
Nothing specific	2	50
Right age	1	25
Total	**4**	**100**

In majority cases of respondents who had delayed marriage, they did not know the specific reason for the delay. Whereas 14.3 per cent said that they had family burdens, 14.2 per cent said the marriage got delayed because of the studies and the need to secure a job (Table 32).

Among those 81 married, 50.6 per cent joined the job after marriage and 49.4 per cent joined before the marriage (Table 33).

Table-32
Reason for Delay in Marriage

Reason for Delay in Marriage	*f*	%
Family burden	2	14.3
No specific reason	10	71.5
Studies	1	7.1
Waited for job	1	7.1
Total	**14**	**100**

Table-33
Joining the Present Job

Joining the Job	*f*	%
After marriage	41	50.6
Before marriage	40	49.4
Total	**81**	**100**

Out of those 41 who joined the job after marriage, 92.7 per cent had husband's consent to join the job. The rest (7.3%) did not get the consent from spouse for the job.

When asked whether the married women get help from spouse for the household chores, 76 of them responded. In the total of 81 married media women, five respondents did not answer the question in which two are widows and three are divorcees. In those 76, 47.4 per cent reported that they obtained the help from the spouse only to some extent, 46 per cent said they received help to a great extent from their spouse and 6.6 per cent do not at all get the help from spouse (Table 34).

Table-34
Spouse's Help in Household Chores

Type of Help	*% (n=76)*
To a great extent	46.0
To some extent	47.4
Not at all	6.6
Total	**100**

Children

Among those 81 married, 53 (65.4%) have children. Of those 53, (56.6%) women respondents gave birth to first child after joining the job. The rest (43.4%) of them gave birth to a child before joining the job itself (Table 35).

Table-35
Time of Birth of First Child

Time of First Child Birth	*% (n=53)*
Before joining the job	43.4
After joining the job	56.6
Total	**100**

Of those 53 respondents who have children, only 14 (20%) women have second child. In those 20 per cent the number of years of gap between the birth of first and second child is also interesting. About 43 per cent opted for a gap of 4-6 years between two children, 28.6 per cent had the gap of 1-3 years and 21.4 per cent took more than 10 years and 7 per cent reported that they had the gap of 7-9 years (Table 36).

Table-36
Gap Between First and Second Child

Gap in Years	*f*	*%*
1-3	4	28.6
4-6	6	42.9
7-9	1	7.1
10 and above	3	21.4
Total	**14**	**100.0**

Among the 14 media women who have a second child, for ten of them the gap between the first and the second child is more than four years. They reported that because of professional pressure they postponed the bearing of the second child. Financial constraints, lack of proper childcare arrangements and other causes contributed for the delay in bearing the second children. 10 per cent said that health was the reason for time gap between two children (Table 37).

Table-37
Reason for Gap Between First and Second Child

Reason for Gap	*% (n=10)*
Health	10.0
Professional pressure	30.0
Financial constraints	20.0
Childcare arrangements	20.0
Any other	20.0
Total	**100**

Childcare Arrangements

The respondents having children have made different types of childcare arrangements. More than half of them (54.4%) depended on relatives for the care of children (Table 38). In the remaining cases, 19.3 per cent went for other types of arrangements, 12.3 per cent each sent them either to crèche or hired some one to take care of the small children. Only one respondent (1.7%) sent the child to nursery.

Table-38
Type of Arrangements Made for Childcare

Childcare Arrangements	*f*	*%*
Crèche	7	12.3
Nursery	1	1.7
Hired some one	7	12.3
Care by relatives	31	54.4
Any other	11	19.3
Total	**57**	**100**

When it came to relative's care to children, many a time parents took care of them. 71 per cent took the support of parents followed by 19.4 per cent who took the help of mother-in-law and one each was supported by husband's relatives, cousin or aunty (Table 39). One of them made more than one arrangement for children's care.

Table-39
Relatives who Take Care of the Respondent's Children

Childcare Arrangements	*f*	%
Parents	22	71.0
Mother in law	6	19.4
Husband relatives	1	3.2
Cousin	1	3.2
Aunty	1	3.2
Total	**31**	**100**

Despite varied types of childcare arrangements, many respondents did not have complete satisfaction about them. Of the 53, about half (49%) of them are somewhat satisfied about the childcare arrangements. 41.5 per cent are very much satisfied, 3.8 per cent are somewhat dissatisfied and another 3.8 per cent are dissatisfied. One respondent reported undecided about the arrangements (Table 40).

Table-40
Level of Satisfaction of the Respondent in Childcare Arrangements

Satisfaction with Childcare Arrangements	*f*	%
Very much satisfied	22	41.5
Some what satisfied	26	49.0
Undecided	1	1.9
Some what dissatisfied	2	3.8
Dissatisfied	2	3.8
Total	**53**	**100**

Among the women who are working in news-related jobs of media organizations, majority get 0-3 hours of time to spend with their children while 30 per cent get between 4-6 hours. Only 12 per cent get more than 6 hours to spend with their children (Table 41).

Table–41
Duration of Time Spent with the Children in a Day

Number of Hours	*% (n=50)*
0–3	58.0
4–6	30.0
6 and above	12.0
Total	**100**

When it comes to comforting the child whenever necessary, in many cases (60.4%) both the respondents and their spouses comforted the children. In 30.2 per cent cases, respondents themselves comforted the children (Table 42). In only a few cases (7.5%) only spouses take the responsibility to comfort the child.

Table–42
Comforting the Children

Response	*f*	%
Self mostly	16	30.2
Self and spouse equally	32	60.4
Spouse mostly	4	7.5
Others (specify)	1	1.9
Total	**53**	**100**

Recreation

The researchers made an attempt to ascertain respondent's participation in family functions. More than three fourths (78%) of the respondents reported that they attend to family functions only to some extent, whereas 18.9 per cent attend to a great extent and 3.1 per cent do not at all go to such functions (Table 43).

Table–43
Attending to Family Functions by the Respondent

Response	*f*	%
To a great extent	24	18.9
To some extent	99	78.0
Not at all	4	3.1
Total	**127**	**100**

Among the total sample of 127, only 64 have responded to the question of visiting parents place. Some of the respondents are staying in the same city and some of them who are unmarried stay with parents themselves. Among those who are away from parents and visit them, half of the respondents said that they visit them more than two times a year. 31.2 per cent visit once in a year and 18.8 per cent visit twice in a year (Table 44).

Table–44
Visit to Parents by the Respondent

Visit to Parents	*f*	%
Once in a year	20	31.2
Twice in a year	12	18.8
More than two times in year	32	50.0
Total	**64**	**100**

To the specific question of how many times they visited their in-laws, only 44 responded (Table 45). Out of the 44, 41 per cent said that they visit in laws more than two times in a year. 29.5 per cent each visit once in a year and twice in a year. They visit their in-laws only on the occasion of festivals and vacations. However, the duration of stay during each visit may vary from a day to few days.

Table-45
Frequency of Visit to in-Laws House

Visit to in-Laws House	*f*	%
Once in a year	13	29.5
Twice in a year	13	29.5
More than two times in a year	18	41.0
Total	**44**	**100**

Type of Engagement

Among the 127 respondents, 31.5 per cent prefer to go for get-togethers on the weekly-off day. 26.8 per cent reported that other types of engagements like visiting parents, household work etc. and 15.0 per cent would like to watch movie on a weekly-off. (Table 46).

Table-46
Type of Engagement of the Respondent During Weekly Off

Type of Engagement	*f*	%
Cinema	19	15.0
Family Outing	16	12.6
Park/Beach	2	1.6
Get-together	40	31.5
Church/Temple /Mosque	5	3.9
Restaurant	5	3.9
Shopping	6	4.7
Any other	34	26.8
Total	**127**	**100**

When asked about outing with husband, 76 of them responded to the question. Among them 31.6 per cent reported that they go out once a week and 30.3 per cent go rarely. About 20 per cent go several times a week (Table 47).

However, 5 (6.6%) respondents never go out with their husband. They are from organizations such as *Visalandhra* (32 years), *All India Radio* (32 years), *Andhra Jyothi* (35 years), *Vaartha* (39 years) and *Prajasakhti* (42 years).

Table–47
Frequency of Outing with Husband by the Respondent

Frequency of Outing with Husband	*f*	%
Never	5	6.6
Rarely	23	30.3
Several times a week	15	19.7
About once a week	24	31.6
Only on special occasions	9	11.8
Total	**76**	**100**

The data pertaining to the study were collected in November, December and January months in which Christmas and New-Year Day holidays fell. Therefore, the respondents reported recreation in the previous weeks. When asked about the time of last recreation, the 127 respondents had enjoyed the last week, 88.2 per cent said that it is less than one week (Table 48). In the rest, 4.7 per cent said they last had it in one week.

When asked about the hobbies of the respondents, about 90 per cent had hobbies and 10 per cent did not have any hobbies. Among those 114 who have hobbies, only 57 per cent have time to develop them. Almost all the respondents reported hobbies such as embroidery, knitting, house decoration and garment stitching for children.

Table-48
The Last Recreation of the Respondent

Last Recreation	*f*	%
Below one week	112	88.2
One week	6	4.7
2- 4 weeks	4	3.2
More than one month	1	0.8
More than three months	4	3.1
Total	**127**	**100**

5

WORKING MEDIA WOMEN AND WORK ENVIRONMENT

This chapter focuses on the employment details of the respondent such as type of appointment, age of joining the service, duration of training and the nature of duties. Further, details related to provision of facilities in the office, professional freedom and so on are presented.

The researchers made an attempt to ascertain information related to employment details of the respondents. The researchers asked the respondents what the designation was when the respondent joined the present organization. Nearly 30 per cent of the respondents reported that they joined the present organization as trainees, while 28 per cent reported that they were working in newspaper organizations as sub-editors prior to joining the present position. However 15 per cent of the respondents started their career as reporters in newspapers. Interestingly 2.4 per cent of the respondents joined the organization as a proofreader, the designation which is not found in any newspaper organization at present. These 2.4 per cent of the respondents joined *Visalandhra,* a leftist newspaper as proofreader. Only one respondent joined the present organization as teleprinter operator (See Table 49).

Appointment

Table 50 describes the type of appointment of the respondents. More (53.5%) than half of the respondents have been appointed permanently in the respective organizations, while,

Table–49
Designation of the Respondent at the Time of Joining the Present Job

Designation when Joined the Present Organization	*f*	%
Trainees	38	29.9
Transmission Executive	2	1.5
Script Writer	1	0.8
Feature Editor	1	0.8
Proof-Reader	3	2.4
Programme Associate	1	0.8
Announcer	3	2.4
Casual Announcer	1	0.8
Bureau Chief	1	0.8
Computer Operator	3	2.4
Radio Jockey	2	1.5
Copy-editor	8	6.3
Sub-editor	36	28.3
Senior Sub-editor	1	0.8
Part time Sub-editor	1	0.8
Reporter	19	15.0
Senior Reporter	3	2.4
Chief Reporter	1	0.8
Programme Executive (AIR)	2	1.5
Total	**127**	**100**

24.4 per cent of the respondents are on contract and 22 per cent have been appointed temporarily. Interestingly, more number of contract employees is found in big media organizations (Table 51). *Times of India* has 7 and its sister publication *Economic Times* has 3 contract employees, *Etv* has employed 6, *AIR* has 4, followed by *New Indian Express, Prajasakhti* and *Andhra Jyothi* with two media women each. *Andhra Bhoomi, Vaartha, TV9, Etv2, The Hindu* have one media woman each on a contract.

Table-50
Type of Appointment of the Respondent

Type of Appointment	*f*	%
Permanent	68	53.5
Contract	31	24.4
Temporary	28	22.1
Total	**127**	**100**

The researchers wanted to ascertain from the respondents how they came to know about the job about 38 per cent reported that they learnt about the job through advertisements (Table 52). While 31.5 per cent of the respondents came to know about the job through friends. Information about the job obtained from various other sources also helped some of them to know about the job. In these other sources, campus recruitments were more in number. Next in this category were personal inquiries, professional contacts and employee references etc. helped some to secure jobs. One media woman was offered a job by the organization itself. Only 11 per cent of them informed that they came to know about the job through relatives. However, about 59 per cent of the respondents joined the present job when they were between 20–25 years while 11 per cent joined the job when they were below 20 years (Table 53).

Duration of Service

Table 55 explains the duration of service of respondents. Interestingly three fourths (74.8%) of the respondents have less than 5 years of experience, while, 20.5 per cent have service between 6–10 years. Moreover 4.7 per cent respondents have more than 11 years of experience.

Table-51
Type of Employment in Media Organizations

Media Organization	*Permanent*		*Temporary*		*Contract*	
	f	%	*f*	%	*f*	%
Newspaper						
Andhra Bhoomi	1	1.5	-	-	1	3.2
Andhra Jyothi	6	8.8	-	-	2	6.5
Deccan Chronicle	1	1.5	2	7.1	-	-
Economic Times	-	-	-	-	3	9.7
Eenadu	10	14.7	1	3.6	-	-
New Indian Express	2	2.9	-	-	2	6.5
Prajasakhti	1	1.5	5	17.8	2	6.5
The Hindu	14	20.6	-	-	1	3.2
Times of India	-	-	1	3.6	7	22.6
Vaartha	3	4.4	4	14.3	1	3.2
Visakha Samacharam	1	1.5	-	-	-	-
Visalandhra	2	2.9	4	14.3	-	-
Television Channel						
Etv	7	10.3	5	17.8	6	19.3
Etv2	4	5.9	2	7.1	1	3.2
Excel	-	-	1	3.6	-	-
TV9	11	16.2	2	7.1	1	3.2
Radio						
All India Radio	5	7.3	1	3.6	4	12.9
Total	**68**	**100**	**28**	**100**	**31**	**100**

Table-52
Source of Information for Joining the Job

Source of Information	*f*	%
Advertisement	49	38.6
Friends	40	31.5
Acquaintances, Campus recruitments etc.	24	18.9
Relatives	14	11.0
Total	**127**	**100**

Table-53
Age of Joining the Job by the Respondent

Age of Joining the Job	*f*	%
Below 20 yrs	14	11.0
20–25	74	58.3
26–30	26	20.5
30+	13	10.2
Total	**127**	**100**

N = 127
Mean age = 34.8 years

Table-54
Age of the Respondent when She Joined the Job in Different Media Organizations

Media Organization	*Below 20*		*20-25*		*26-30*		*Above 30*	
	f	%	*f*	%	*f*	%	*f*	%
Newspaper								
Andhra Bhoomi	-	-	1	1.4	1	3.8	-	-
Andhra Jyothi	-	-	2	2.7	2	7.7	4	30.8
Deccan Chronicle	1	7.1	1	1.4	1	3.8	-	-
Economic Times	-	-	2	2.7	1	3.8	-	-
Eenadu	1	7.1	7	9.4	2	7.7	1	7.7

Contd...

Media Organization	*Below 20*		*20-25*		*26-30*		*Above 30*	
	f	%	*f*	%	*f*	%	*f*	%
New Indian Express	-	-	4	5.4	-	-	-	-
Prajasakhti	2	14.4	4	5.4	-	-	2	15.3
The Hindu	2	14.4	7	9.4	2	7.7	4	30.8
Times of India	-	-	6	8.1	2	7.7	-	-
Vaartha	1	7.1	2	2.7	5	19.3	-	-
Visakha Samacharam	-	-	1	1.4	-	-	-	-
Visalandhra	1	7.1	4	5.4	1	3.8	-	-
Television Channel								
Etv	1	7.1	16	21.6	-	-	1	7.7
Etv2	-	-	5	6.8	2	7.7	-	-
Excel	-	-	-	-	1	3.8	-	-
TV9	4	28.6	8	10.8	1	3.8	1	7.7
Radio								
All India Radio	1	7.1	4	5.4	5	19.3	-	-
Total	**14**	**100**	**74**	**100**	**26**	**100**	**13**	**100**

Table–55
Distribution of Respondents According to Duration of Service

Duration of Service	*f*	%
Below 5 years	95	74.8
6-10 years	26	20.5
11-15 years	4	3.2
Above 15 years	2	1.5
Total	**127**	**100**

Motivation Factor

When the important factors in journalism are journalists, their perceptions of their role in society are very important. If they perceive journalism as a profession for the public welfare, the profession sets two standards (Soloski, 1989): (1) It sets standards and norms of behaviour, and (2) it determines the professional reward system. Studies did in two different settings reveal the perceptions of their role. An Indian study found a large number of trained journalists was of the view that journalists sacrifice public interest if it clashes with their self interest. Most of the journalists exploit their status for non-journalistic purposes (Sharma, 1990). Further, the study found that 9.6 per cent of the journalists reported that journalism is meant for public service. The study reveled that sensationalism had become a practice in journalism, and sometimes sensationalism was practiced in the name of investigative journalism. It helps the journalists and newspapers, while journalists achieve fame and personal gains in their career, since newspapers achieve larger circulations. In contrast, the American study found that a majority (60%) of journalists now say the editorial policies of their organizations are very important in how they rate their job (Weaver and Wilhoit, 1997). The study also found the chance to help people remains a very important aspect of news work for a majority (61%), but altruism is somewhat more apt to be cited by journalists, especially by minority journalists in broadcasting and weekly newspapers than other media.

Table 56 shows the details of factor that motivated the respondents to join the job. 21.3 per cent reported that the motivation factor was a scope to express views, followed by 19.6 per cent who expressed that the chance to help others/ reform the society motivated them to join the profession. However, only 5.2 per cent of them reported that salary was the motivation factor while 3 per cent joined the job because of unemployment.

Training

As discussed earlier, media women are defined as a woman working in a mass communication channel related to gathering, editing, producing and anchoring of messages. Therefore, in order to carry out media related jobs, a formal

Table-56
Factor that Motivated Respondents to Join Media Organizations

Motivation Factor	*f*	%
Scope to express views	49	21.3
Chance to help others/Reform the society	45	19.6
To avoid monotonous jobs	37	16.1
It was accidental and opportunity has come her way	30	13.1
Scope to move up quickly	21	9.1
Recognition/Power/Prestige	18	7.8
Salary	12	5.2
Witness to history	11	4.8
Unemployment/No choice	7	3.0
Total	**230**	**100**

N = 127

Note: Since the respondents have given multiple responses, the total does not tally with N.

training is a basic necessity to understand the policy of the channel as well as the nature of the job. Hence a question was posed to the respondent as to whether formal training was given to her or not. In the study sample of 127, only 63.8 per cent of the respondents were given training. Mostly, these respondents were from 12 newspapers and 4 TV channels.

The duration of the training varied from one month to one year. In the study, about 48 per cent of the respondents were given training for more than 6 months. These respondents were from newspapers such as *Eenadu, Times of India, Vaartha, New Indian Express* and others, whereas 43 per cent of the respondents underwent training between four and six months (Table 57).

Table-57
Duration of Training of the Respondent

Duration of Training	*f*	%
1–3 months	7	8.6
4–6 months	35	43.2
6–12 months	39	48.2
Total	**81**	**100**

Since respondents were trained in the respective media channels, they were given regular duty. Most (71.6%) of the respondents were sent to regular duty such as editing and anchoring, while 27.6 per cent were sent out for reporting (Table 58).

Table-58
Type of Work Given to Respondent in the Organization

Work Given After Training	*f*	%
Beat	35	27.6
Regular duty	91	71.6
Features	1	0.8
Total	**127**	**100**

Out of these 35 respondents who were given different beats, 34 per cent of them were given general reporting and education (Table 59). Interestingly, 8.6 per cent of the respondents were given specialized, male dominated area i.e., crime news. There is one respondent who was given automobile industry. The reporters who were given crime beat were from *TV9* and *Deccan Chronicle*. One respondent from *Economic Times* was given a task to cover automobile industry. *TV9* has more women reporters compared to other media organizations and the range of beats is also highly varied. The beats which were allotted to these reporters were general, current affairs, crime, education, politics and daily features. Generally crime and politics are considered to be male dominated beats. No other media organization has entrusted the beat to cover politics to the women reporters. *Eenadu* which is the biggest newspaper organization has two women reporters who cover issues related to women and youth. The same is the case with the other big newspaper organizations like *The Hindu* and *Times of India*. The two women reporters in *The Hindu* were allocated education and city life, while the five reporters in *Times of India* cover education, health and general reporting.

Table–59
Type of Beat Given to the Reporters in the Sample

Type of Beat	*f*	%
Agriculture	2	5.7
Art	1	2.9
Automobiles	1	2.9
General	6	17.0
Education	6	17.0
Business	2	5.7
Crime	3	8.6
Current Affairs	1	2.9
Entertainment	1	2.9
Features	3	8.6
Youth Affairs	1	2.9
Health	1	2.9
International	2	5.7
Life Style	1	2.9
Politics	2	5.7
Tourism	1	2.9
Women	1	2.9
Total	**35**	**100**

N = 127

Shift Duty

As the work of a media woman is rigorous and the round the clock, three fourths of the respondents work in shift duties which vary in timings. In request of the media channel, the shift timings are varied. In the context of globalization, women in media are coming forward to work in the media even after late hours. Therefore it is found in the present study that more than half of the respondents work in night shifts (Table 60). These respondents are from TV networks and newspaper organizations such as *Etv, TV9, Eenadu, The Hindu* etc.

Table-60
Shift Timings of Respondent

Shift Timings	*f*	%
10am–5pm	15	15.6
2–9pm	19	19.8
5–12pm	10	10.4
Day shift/night shift	31	32.3
Complete night shift	21	21.9
Total	**96**	**100**

However, when media women work in the night shifts, transport from the office to the home is increasingly becoming a problem. Around 40 per cent of the respondents do not get transport provided by the office.

Further, as can be seen from Table 61, nearly 17 per cent of the respondents reported that they could get transport only on demand, while 35 per cent get transport only on request, while 25.9 per cent respondents reported that transport was provided by the organizations as a policy for all the respondents who are working in the night shift. Moreover, when they are in the day shifts, transport is not provided by the organization.

Table-61
Provision of Transport to the Respondent

Provision of Transport	*f*	%
On request	27	35.1
On demand	13	16.9
Self	17	22.1
Policy of the organization	20	25.9
Total	77	**100**

Work for Extra Hours

In mass communication channels, media personnel are expected to meet the deadlines; hence they have to work for the purpose. In the process of completing the task in hand, the media personnel are subjected to pressure of work because unforeseen circumstances arise in the last leg of the work. Therefore, 87.4 per cent of the respondents take up extra work. Specifically for the working journalists, the Working Journalists (Working Conditions) Act, 1955 stipulates 6 hours of work in the day hours and 5.5 hours in the night hours. Contrary to this Act, the working journalists work beyond the hours. The reasons are obvious.

A majority (44%) of the respondents reported shortage of staff in the office for the extra work, while 17.2 per cent of the respondents cited the reason of publishing special supplements for special occasions. An insignificant percentage (2.6%) of respondents reported lack of cooperation from the colleagues for extra work (Table 62).

However 111 respondents reported working for extra hours in the office, only 36 per cent are paid for extra work. Out of these 36 per cent of the respondents, 57.5 per cent of the respondents are given compensatory leaves, while 30 per cent of the respondents are paid money for the extra work (Table 63).

Table–62
Reason for Extra Work in the Organization

Reason	*f*	%
Shortage of staff	51	44.0
Lack of cooperation	3	2.6
Lack of inputs like stories, news	11	9.5
Frequent special events	18	15.5
Special occasions like special supplements	20	17.2
Any other	13	11.2
Total	**116***	**100**

* *Note:* Three respondents have given multiple responses.

Table–63
Mode of Payment for Extra Hours

Mode of Payment for Extra Hours	*f*	%
Money	12	30.0
Compensatory leave	23	57.5
Any other	3	7.5
Money/compensatory leave	2	5.0
Total	**40**	**100**

Added to the extra work, the respondents were asked a specific question whether the respondents carried office work home, about 60 per cent of the respondents do not carry office work to home, whereas 39.4 per cent of the respondents reported that they carry office work to home "to some extent", and a negligible percentage of respondent carry office work to home "to a large extent" (Table 64).

To another question, "would the respondents be paid money for special assignments" about 31 per cent of the respondents were paid money for special assignments.

Table-64
Degree of Office Work Being Carried by Respondents to Home

Office Work at Home	*f*	%
To a great extent	2	1.6
To some extent	50	39.4
Not at all	75	59.0
Total	**127**	**100**

Facilities at Work Place

As regards facilities, childcare arrangements were not available in any of those media organizations (Table 65). Even in the government controlled media organizations like *All India Radio,* the childcare arrangements were not available at the work place. About 15 per cent of the respondents reported a grievance cell was set up in the organization. These organizations include *All India Radio, Etv, Etv2, Eenadu, New Indian Express, The Hindu, Times of India, Prajasakhti* and *Visalandhra.*

Table-65
Facilities Provided in the Office for the Respondents

Facilities	*f*	%
Toilets	127	100
Drinking water	124	97.6
Rest rooms	43	33.8
Childcare	-	-
Canteen	108	85.0
Grievance cell	20	15.7
Recreation club	19	14.9

Additional Provisions

As part of their profession, respondents are entitled for additional provisions such as accreditation, health insurance and professional membership. Mostly respondents' working in newspapers and television channels derive these additional facilities associated with the profession. For instance, accreditation entails respondents for government incentives such as tours with dignitaries, concessional travel for long distance and lands for subsidized rates etc. Therefore, journalists are keen on becoming accredited journalists. Earlier, the newspaper managements recommended a select staff for accreditation. Hence, the present study makes an attempt to ascertain how many media women have been recommended for such a provision from the managements. Only 21.1 per cent of respondents have got an accreditation (Table 66). About 61.9 per cent had health insurance and 17 per cent of them are members of professional bodies.

Table-66
Additional Provisions Given by the Managements

Additional Provisions	*f*	%
Accreditation	31	21.1
Health insurance	91	61.9
Any other professional membership	25	17.0
Total	**147**	**100**

Wage Boards

Do media organizations implement wage board? The Central Government sets up wage boards for newspaper journalists to review wage structure. However, television channels do not come under the ambit of wage boards, and the respective managements of television networks implement the wages regardless of the government wage boards. Thus, 36.2 per cent of respondents reported that their managements implement wage boards. These organizations include *All India Radio, Deccan Chronicle, Andhra Jyothi, Andhra Bhoomi, The Hindu, New Indian Express, Times of India, Etv, Eenadu, Visalandhra, Prajasakhti,* and *TV9.*

The big newspapers, as a mandatory principle/policy implement wage boards. But, small newspapers such as *Visakha Samacharam* do not implement wage board.

When asked about providing insurance for risk coverage, half of the respondents said that they were not provided with the facility. Only 26.8 per cent of the respondents informed that they had this facility (Table 67).

Table-67
Provision of Insurance for Risk Coverage by Management

Insurance for Risk Coverage	*f*	%
Yes	34	26.8
No	67	52.8
Cannot say	26	20.4
Total	**127**	**100**

Availing of Leave

In relation to sanctioning of leave by the management, more (54.3%) than half of the respondents obtain leave when applied, while 44 per cent of them obtain leave "to some extent" and 1.6 per cent of them do not obtain leave when applied (Table 68). Further, about 41 per cent of respondents avail of leave rarely, while half (50.4%) of them reported less frequently in availing of leave and 8.7 per cent of them reported availing of leave frequently (Table 69).

Table-68
Sanctioning of Leave by Managements

Sanction of Leave	*f*	%
To a great extent	69	54.3
To some extent	56	44.1
Not at all	2	1.6
Total	**127**	**100**

Table-69
Frequency of Leave Availing by Respondents

Availing of Leave	*f*	%
Frequently	11	8.7
Less frequently	64	50.4
Rarely	52	40.9
Total	**127**	**100**

Furthermore, the researcher ascertained the chief reason for availing of leave. A majority (37.8%) of them reported sickness as the main reason for availing of leave, while 23.6 per cent of them reported family or relative's function. Less percentage (9.4%) of them reported festivals in availing of leave (Table 70).

Table-70
Chief Reason for Availing of Leave by Respondents

Chief Reason	*f*	%
Sickness	48	37.8
Children's work	15	11.8
Festivals	12	9.4
Family or relatives functions	30	23.6
Recreation	11	8.7
Any other	11	8.7
Total	**127**	**100**

As regards maternity leave more than (54.3%) half of them reported that management would sanction maternity leave and 37 per cent reported, "can not say" (Table 71).

Work Place Environment

Work place environment is one of the reasons for comfortable working and various studies done in different settings have provided ample evidence to the fact that job satisfaction is also

Table-71
Sanctioning of Maternity Leave

Sanction of Maternity Leave	*f*	%
Yes	69	54.3
No	11	8.7
Cannot say	47	37.0
Total	**127**	**100**

linked to work place environment. For instance, Miller and Miller (1995) explored the experiences of women journalists working in sports, focusing on four areas of potential problems: Condescension in the workplace, equal opportunity in the workplace, perceived performance, and job satisfaction. The results indicate that although females are appearing in sports newsrooms across USA in increasing numbers, women feel they are, "in many ways, invisible to their colleagues, expected to know less and accept more menial assignments, while being the target of sexist language." In spite of the discrimination approximately three fourths of the respondents said that they were satisfied with their jobs.

In another study Daniels and Hollifield (2002) studied short and long term effects of organizational change on newsroom employees in which they found that for newsroom managers, organizational change was a losing proposition, resulting in staff member's perception of great unhappiness with their jobs. Newsroom employees were most negative about changes they thought hindered their ability to provide high quality journalists, and change management efforts had only limited impact on job satisfaction and commitment. The study examined short and long term effects of 1998 series of changes in the CNN Headline News Organization On Headline News personnel changes: The changes involved personnel, technology, work schedules, work processes, and news formats. The study, conducted across 15 months, examined how newsroom employees responded to the specific changes and their overall effects on job satisfaction, attitude towards managements and commitment to the job. Studies examining specific types of changes, primarily technological, on newsroom employees have found that new technologies can change job roles, require new skills (Russial and Wanta, 1998) increase time spent on technology use and decrease time available to develop content (Russial, 1994). Against this background, the present study ascertained the perceptions of respondents in relation to workplace environment.

Thus, 46.5 per cent of respondents reported that the work place environment is "to a great extent encouraging", while 43.3 per cent of them felt the work place environment is "to some extent encouraging". Whereas, 10.2 per cent reported that it is "not at all encouraging" (Table 72).

Table-72
Respondent's Perception of Work Environment in Office

Work Environment in Office	*f*	%
To a great extent encouraging	59	46.5
To some extent encouraging	55	43.3
Not at all encouraging	13	10.2
Total	**127**	**100**

In terms of individual respondents, a considerable percentage of respondents from *Vaartha, Eenadu, The Hindu* and *Visakha Samacharam* felt that work environment is "to a great extent encouraging." While significant number of respondents from *TV9, Etv* and *Visalandhra* reported that work environment is "to some extent encouraging." Moreover, a significant percentage of respondents from *All India Radio* reported that work environment is "not at all encouraging" (Table 73).

Table-73
Work Environment as Perceived by the Respondent

Media Organization	*Work Environment in the Office*		
	To a Great Extent Encouraging (n=59)	*To Some Extent Encouraging (n=56)*	*Not at all Encouraging (n=12)*
Newspaper			
Andhra Bhoomi	-	3.6	-
Andhra Jyothi	6.8	7.1	-
Deccan Chronicle	1.7	3.6	-
Economic Times	5.1	-	-
Eenadu	11.9	7.1	-
New Indian Express	5.1	1.8	-
Prajasakhti	5.1	8.9	-
The Hindu	11.9	1.1	16.7
Times of India	8.5	4.0	-
Vaartha	3.4	8.9	8.32
Visakha Samacharam	1.7	-	-
Visalandhra	8.5	1.8	-
Television Channel			
Etv	10.2	12.5	41.7
Etv2	1.7	7.1	16.6
Excel	1.7	-	-
TV9	8.5	16.1	-
Radio			
All India Radio	8.5	5.4	16.7
Total	**100**	**100**	**100**

Do Working Women Face Problems in the Office?

In order to ascertain the attitude of working women as to whether they face problems in the office a 4-point scale was used. More (50.4%) than half of the respondents reported that they do not believe working women face problems in the office, whereas the other half of them reported that they believe women face problems. The degree of their belief has varied. 16.5 per cent of them reported "less belief" for the question of working women face problems whereas 18.1 per cent felt that they "believe" and 15 per cent of them reported "strongly believe" that working women face problems in the office (Table 74).

Table-74
Working Women Face Problems

Working Women Face Problems	*f*	%
Strongly believe	19	15.0
Believe	23	18.1
Less believe	21	16.5
Do not believe	64	50.4
Total	**127**	**100**

In terms of their designation, it is seen more (57.5%) than half of the reporters reported that they do not believe that working women face problems. Likewise, 47.5 per cent of sub editors also reported that they do not believe that working women face problems in the office (Table 75).

In respect of different media, more (61.3%) than half of the respondents from print media reported that they do not face problems in the office. Further, more (65.4%) than half of the respondents from electronic media believe that working women face problems in the office. But, their belief varied from "less believe" to "strongly believe" (Table 76).

However, the researcher further asked them to describe the type of problem faced by working women in the office.

Out of the 54 respondents who believe that women face problems in the office, 31.4 per cent of them described it as lack of cooperation. Three types of other problems were described by the respondents. They are too much of work (16.7%), passing of comments by peers (16.7%) and extended night shift duties (16.7%) (See Table 77).

Table-75

Nature of Job and Working Women Problems in Office

Working Women Face Problems	*Nature of job*		
	Reporter (n=33) %	*Sub editor (n=78) %*	*Others (n=16) %*
Strongly believe	9.1	14.1	31.2
Believe	15.2	19.2	18.7
Less believe	18.2	19.2	-
Do not believe	57.5	47.5	50
Total	**100.0**	**100.0**	**100.0**

Table-76

Women Facing Problems in Media Organizations

Working Women Face Problems	*Media Organization*	
	Electronic (n=52) %	*Print (n=75)* %
Strongly believe	19.2	12.0
Believe	23.1	14.7
Less believe	23.1	12.0
Do not believe	34.6	61.3
Total	**100.0**	**100.0**

Table-77
Type by Problems Being Faced by Respondent in the Office

Type of Problem	*f*	%
Lack of cooperation	17	31.4
Too much of work	9	16.7
Passing of comments by peers	9	16.7
Extended night shift duties	9	16.7
Discrimination from management	8	14.8
Abuse by superiors	2	3.7
Total	**54**	**100.0**

Treatment by Male Colleagues

In a work environment, studies report that gender discrimination is prevalent, and men subject women employees to different kinds of treatment. In the present study, it is found that 40.2 per cent respondents reported that their male colleagues treat them very good, while 32.2 per cent reported that the male colleagues treat them as they treat other men, whereas, 16.5 per cent found their male colleagues are kind and understanding. However, a few respondents reported that their male colleagues show resentment and nasty behaviour (1.6%) and indifferently (7.9%) (Table 78).

Table-78
Treatment Meted out to Respondent by Male Colleagues

Treatment by Male Colleagues	*f*	%
Very good	51	40.2
Treat us just as they treat men	41	32.2
Kind and understanding	21	16.5
Resentful and nasty	2	1.6
Indifferent	10	7.9
Good	2	1.6
Total	**127**	**100**

Specifically, respondents from *Etv* and *TV9* reported that the male colleagues are resentful and nasty, while respondents from three newspapers *Prajasakhti, Times of India* and *The Hindu,* and three TV channels *Etv, Etv2* and *TV9* reported that their male colleagues are indifferent toward them (Table 79).

Table-79
Treatment of Respondents by Male Colleagues in Organizations

Media Organization	*Very Good (n=51)*	*Treat as Men (n=40)*	*Kind and Under-standing (n=22)*	*Resentful and Nasty (n=2)*	*Indifferent (n=10)*	*Good (n=2)*
	%	%	%	%	%	%
Newspaper						
Andhra Bhoomi	-	5.0	-	-	-	-
Andhra Jyothi	7.9	5.0	9.1	-	-	-
Deccan Chronicle	5.9	-	-	-	-	-
Economic Times	3.9	2.5	-	-	-	-
Eenadu	3.9	12.5	18.2	-	-	-
New Indian Express	1.9	7.5	-	-	-	-
Prajasakhti	9.8	2.5	4.5	-	10	-
The Hindu	9.8	15.0	9.1	-	20	-
Times of India	1.9	12.5	-	-	20	-
Vaartha	3.9	10.0	9.1			
Visakha Samacharam	1.9	-	-	-	-	-
Visalandhra	11.9	-	-	-	-	-
Television Channel						
Etv	9.8	7.5	27.3	50	30	100
Etv2	5.9	5.0	4.5	-	10	-
Excel	1.9	-	-	-	-	-
TV9	13.8	7.5	9.1	50	10	-
Radio						
All India Radio	5.9	7.5	9.1		-	
Total	**100**	**100**	**100**	**100**	**100**	**100**

6

WORKING MEDIA WOMEN AND JOB SATISFACTION

Research on job satisfaction stretches more than five decades (Herzberg *et al.*, 1959) making it one of the most frequently studied variables in research on organizations behaviour (Spector, 1997). Interest in the concept has come both from scholars and managers. Some times that research has been based on humanistic concerns. For example, studies have looked at the influence of job satisfaction on individual's quality of life or sense of wellbeing (Kalleberg, 1974). More often, however, practical considerations have motivated researchers' interests; job satisfaction can influence job commitment, turnover, productivity and other factors that affect the successful operation of an organization (Spector, 1997). In the early 1960s, Vroom (1964) noted that: "Job satisfaction" and "job attitudes" seemed to be used interchangeably since both refer to the affective orientation of the individual toward the work role he is occupying. Later, Carroll (1973) defined job satisfaction as the evaluation of one's job.

Scholars have disagreed about whether job satisfaction and dissatisfaction are separate constructs of simply different sides of the same conceptual coin. Others have argued that job satisfaction and job dissatisfaction are different concepts (Herzberg *et al.*, 1959). They say job satisfaction is affected by factors such as the work itself, recognition, responsibilities, achievement, and advancement, while job dissatisfaction on the other hand is a function of things like pay, administration, company policy, relationships with colleagues, and working environment. Presumably, a worker could be simultaneously satisfied and dissatisfied with a job. Nevertheless, job satisfaction has been tracked regularly since 1971 through decennial surveys of U.S. journalists and occasional studies by professional associations (Voakes, 1997). For example, a 2001 *Columbia Journalism Review* article, reported that 84 per cent of those in a self selected survey of 127 journalists said employee morale was low (Hickey, 2001). Strupp (2004) reported that the paper's newsroom had moral problems that were, in part the result of corporate owners desire to make the publication more profitable.

Pollard (1995) looked at another source of tension: The conflict between occupational and organizational values. He proposed that two control centers govern journalists in complex organizations–the profession and the organization. Each has its own values, which are sometimes at odds. He found that journalists were more satisfied with their jobs if they had more autonomy, authority, and control. Finally, Stamm and Underwood (1993) explored the impact of organizational policies on journalist's job satisfaction. They surveyed 429 news staffers at 12 West Coast dailies in USA and found that perception about the business and journalistic goals of the employed affected job satisfaction. If journalistic quality was perceived to be increasing, job satisfaction was higher, but if business goals were perceived to be hurting quality, job satisfaction suffered.

Demers (1994) examined the impact of organizational size on job satisfaction among top editors at US dailies. Arguing that one's position within the organization's hierarchy would affect the relationship between organization size and job satisfaction. He hypothesized that this relationship would be conditional for non-managers and size would be positively related. His research did not test that proposed difference, but he did find their counterparts at smaller papers, though that relationship was not linear. Berkowitz (1993) studied whether two different organizational roles of being a TV producer and being a TV reporter or anchor were associated with different perceptions of journalistic values and attitudes toward work. TV news workers who most strongly believe the journalistic values guide news choices (as opposed to programming or resource considerations) had the highest satisfaction with their jobs.

Miller and Miller (1995) in their study observed that approximately three fourths of the respondents reported that they were either very satisfied or fairly satisfied with their jobs. However, respondents also tended to say that their news organizations had glass ceiling in place for women in sports. In addition to problems women face in office, sexism, unequal opportunity, and a lack of respect from colleague, respondents also gave traditional dislikes about the job, low pay ranked first, followed by long hours and a dysfunctional lifestyle. Fewer respondents listed high profile professional beats like foot ball, base ball, hockey, basket ball and golf. 56 per cent reported a change of job within the past five years, 42 per cent reported moving to a large organization, and 49 per cent reported receiving a pay increase over three years.

Against this backdrop the present study made an attempt to ascertain the job satisfaction levels of the working media women. Out of 127 respondents, nearly 69 per cent of the total respondents have expressed satisfaction, and 18 per cent of the total respondents were very satisfied with their job. A negligible percentage (0.8%) of the respondents is very much dissatisfied with the job (Table 80, Table 81 and also Figure 2). This respondent is from *Vaartha* newspaper. However, 5.5 per cent of the total respondents are dissatisfied with the job. They belong to *Etv, Etv2, Prajasakhti, The Hindu* and *Vaartha.* Further examination reveals that married women were dissatisfied and very much dissatisfied with the job (Table 82).

Table-80
Level of Job Satisfaction Reported by Respondent

Level of Satisfaction	*f*	%
Very much satisfied	23	18.1
Satisfied	87	68.5
Dissatisfied	7	5.5
Very much dissatisfied	1	0.8
Can't say	9	7.1
Total	**127**	**100**

Table-81
Job Satisfaction Levels of Respondents from Different Organizations

Media Organization	*Satisfaction with the Present Job*				
	Very Much Satisfied (n=23)	*Satisfied (n=87)*	*Dissatisfied (n=7)*	*Very Much Dissatisfied (n=1)*	*Can't Say (n=9)*
	%	%	%	%	%
Newspaper					
Andhra Bhoomi	4.34	1.14	-	-	-
Andhra Jyothi	4.34	5.75	-	-	22.22
Deccan Chronicle	-	1.14	-	-	22.22
Economic Times	-	3.45	-	-	-
Eenadu	8.69	10.34	-	-	-
New Indian Express	4.34	3.45	-	-	-
Prajasakhti	4.34	6.89	14.28	-	-
The Hindu	13.04	12.64	14.28	-	-
Times of India	-	8.05	-	-	11.11
Vaartha	-	6.89	14.28	100	-

Contd...

Media Organization	Satisfaction with the Present Job				
	Very Much Satisfied (n=23)	Satisfied (n=87)	Dissatisfied (n=7)	Very Much Dissatisfied (n=1)	Can't Say (n=9)
	%	%	%	%	%
Visakha Samacharam	4.34	-	-	-	-
Visalandhra	8.69	4.59	-	-	-
Television Channel					
Etv	-	16.09	28.57	-	22.22
Etv2	4.34	3.45	28.57	-	11.11
Excel TV	-	1.14	-	-	-
TV9	26.08	8.05	-	-	11.11
Radio					
All India Radio	17.39	6.89	-	-	-
Total	**100**	**100**	**100**	**100**	**100**

N = 127

Table-82
Marital Status and Job Satisfaction of Respondent

Marital Status	Satisfaction with Present Job (n=127)					
	Very Much Satisfied	Satisfied	Dissatis-fied	Very Much Dissatisfied	Can't say	Total
	%	%	%	%	%	%
Married (*n* = 79)	20.0	68.0	4.0	3.0	5.0	100
Unmarried (*n* = 46)	15.2	67.4	8.7	-	8.7	100
Widow (*n* = 2)	-	50	-	-	50	100

More over the reasons for job satisfaction are: producing matters of significance (22.0%), matters which make an impact (19.7%), opportunity to be creative (37.0%), recognition (13.4%), salary (6.3%), working with others in the newsroom (1.6%) (See Table 83).

Table-83

Reason for Job Satisfaction as Reported by the Respondent

Reason for Job Satisfaction	*f*	%
Producing matters of significance	28	22.0
Matters which make an impact	25	19.7
Opportunity to be creative	47	37.0
Recognition	17	13.4
Salary	8	6.3
Working with others in newsroom	2	1.6
Total	**127**	**100**

The Chi square analysis shows that the job satisfaction of respondents did not show significant differences (x^2= 0.9974 p<0.5 df=64).

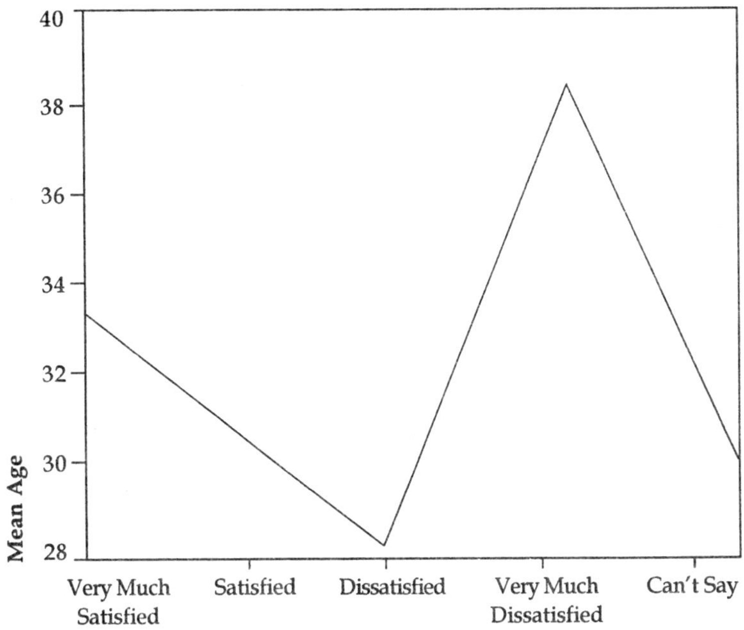

Figure 2: Shows the Decreasing Curve of Job Satisfaction in Relation to Age

In addition to the job satisfaction, above 91 per cent of the respondents reported that they had received appreciation to their work. Most of these respondents reported that they received appreciation from their peers (41.4%) first followed by their management (30.1%) and readers (28.5%) (See Table 84).

Table–84
Source of Appreciation Received by the Respondent

Source of Appreciation	*f*	%
From management	56	30.1
From peers	77	41.4
From readers	53	28.5
Total	**186**	**100**

Promotion

Apart from appreciation, another question of how many of the respondents obtained promotion was also posed to the respondents. Out of 127, only 42 (33.1%) respondents obtained promotion (Table 85).

Table–85
Number of Respondent's who Obtained Promotions in their Organization

Media Organization	*Yes*		*No*	
	f	%	*f*	%
Newspapers				
Andhra Bhoomi	1	2.4	1	1.2
Andhra Jyothi	2	4.8	6	7.1
Deccan Chronicle	2	4.8	1	1.2
Economic Times	3	7.1	-	-
Eenadu	1	2.4	10	11.8
New Indian Express	2	4.8	2	2.3
Prajasakhti	2	4.8	6	7.1

Contd...

Media Organization	*Yes*		*No*	
	f	%	*f*	%
The Hindu	7	16.6	8	9.4
Times of India	3	7.1	5	5.8
Vaartha	1	2.4	7	8.2
Visakha Samacharam	1	2.4	-	-
Visalandhra	2	4.8	4	4.7
Television Channel				
Etv	6	14.2	12	14.1
Etv2	2	4.8	5	5.9
Excel	-	-	1	1.2
TV9	3	7.1	11	12.9
Radio				
All India Radio	4	9.5	6	7.1
Total	**42**	**100**	**85**	**100**

N = 127

Further inquiry revealed that out of these 42, only 25 (59.5%) respondents obtained promotion only once in their career, while one respondent each obtained four and five promotions during their career (Table 86).

Table-86
Number of Promotions Obtained by the Respondent During her Service

Number of Promotions	*f*	%
Once	25	59.5
Twice	10	23.8
Thrice	5	11.9
Four times	1	2.4
Five times	1	2.4
Total	**42**	**100**

Further, the respondents reported the reasons for promotion such as competence (19%), seniority (16.7%) and good work (16.7%) (See Table 87).

Table-87
Reason Reported by the Respondent to Obtain Promotion

Reason	*f*	%
Capability	2	4.8
Commitment	1	2.4
Competence	8	19.0
Nothing specific	4	9.5
Efficiency	6	14.2
Experience	3	7.1
Good work	7	16.7
Hard work	2	4.8
Performance	2	4.8
Seniority	7	16.7
Total	**42**	**100**

On the other hand, those 85 respondents who did not receive promotion reported various other reasons. Prominently, 36.5 per cent of the respondents couldn't give the reason for not obtaining the promotion, followed by 24.7 per cent respondents who believed that less experience was the reason for not getting promotion. However, only one respondent felt that she did not obtain promotion because she was a lady (Table 88).

Story Idea

Mostly, the respondents have been engaged in the creative side of the profession where they produce, edit, and report and anchor programmes. Out of a total of 127 respondents, 102 respondents are directly related to the production of messages or story idea. Therefore, the present study has made

Table-88
Reason Reported by Respondent for not Obtaining Promotion

Reason	*f*	%
Cannot say	31	36.5
Less experience	21	24.7
No specific reason	16	18.8
Management policy	6	7.0
Jealous colleagues	4	4.7
No idea	3	3.5
Because of contract job	1	1.2
No recognition for talent	1	1.2
Discrimination	1	1.2
Being a lady	1	1.2
Total	**85**	**100**

an attempt to ascertain the degree of freedom the respondent in enjoying in producing the messages. Half (50%) of the respondents reported that they always had the opportunity to report new story idea. Above 9 per cent got a rare opportunity to report, while 4 per cent never got the opportunity to report story idea (Table 89).

Table-89
Frequency of Opportunity to Report Story Idea

Frequency to Report Story Idea	*f*	%
Always	51	50.0
Very often	38	37.3
Rarely	9	8.8
Never	4	3.9
Total	**102**	**100**

In deciding an angle of the story about 42 per cent reported almost complete freedom to decide the angle of the story whereas 36 per cent had a great deal of freedom to decide the angle of the story (Table 90).

In 17.3 per cent cases, the respondents have "somewhat" freedom to decide the angle of the story. In relation to specific media organizations most of the respondents from *The Hindu* (18%), *Etv2* (18.2%), *TV9* (22.8%) have expressed that they have "somewhat" freedom to decide the angle of the story (Table 91). The responses given by the respondents from different organizations for freedom of selection of story idea did not show significant differences ($x^2 = 0.5592$, $p < 0.5$, df = 48).

Table-90
Degree of Freedom Given by the Superiors to Decide the Angle of the Story

Response	*f*	%
Almost complete freedom	53	41.8
A great deal	46	36.2
Some what	22	17.3
None	6	4.7
Total	**127**	**100**

Table-91
Degree of Freedom to Select Story Idea Enjoyed by the Respondent in Media Organization

Media Organization	*Almost*		*Great Deal*		*Some What*		*None*	
	f	%	*f*	%	*f*	%	*f*	%
Newspaper								
Andhra Bhoomi	-	-	1	2.2	1	4.5	-	-
Andhra Jyothi	4	7.5	4	8.7	-	-	-	-
Deccan Chronicle	2	3.8	-	-	-	-	1	16.7

Contd...

Media Organization	*Almost*		*Great deal*		*Some what*		*None*	
	f	%	*f*	%	*f*	%	*f*	%
Economic Times	2	3.8	1	2.2	-	-	-	-
Eenadu	5	9.5	6	13.0	-	-	-	-
New Indian Express	3	5.6	1	2.2	-	-	-	-
Prajasakhti	4	7.5	2	4.3	2	9.1	-	-
The Hindu	6	11.3	5	10.9	4	18.2	-	-
Times of India	3	5.7	5	10.9	-	-	-	-
Vaartha	3	5.7	2	4.3	2	9.1	1	16.7
Visakha Samacharam	1	1.9	0	-	-	-	-	-
Visalandhra	3	5.7	2	4.3	1	4.5	-	–
Television Channel								
Etv	6	11.3	8	17.4	2	9.1	2	33.3
Etv2	-	-	1	2.2	4	18.2	2	33.3
Excel	1	1.9	-	-	-	-	-	-
TV9	4	7.5	5	10.9	5	22.8	-	-
Radio								
All India Radio	6	11.3	3	6.5	1	4.5	-	-
Total	**53**	**100**	**46**	**100**	**22**	**100**	**6**	**100**

Evaluation of Work

Is respondent's work evaluated? In 64.6 per cent cases, the work of the respondents is evaluated and 16.5 per cent cases, the work is evaluated sometimes (Table 92).

Next, how frequently the work of the respondents is evaluated? More (52.4%) than half of the respondents work is evaluated every month while in 24.3 per cent cases, their work is evaluated for every three months. However, in 18.4 per cent cases, their work is evaluated for every year (Table 93).

Table–92
Work Evaluation of the Respondent

Response	*f*	%
Yes, frequently	82	64.6
No	24	18.9
Some times	21	16.5
Total	**127**	**100**

With regard to two newspapers an English daily *Deccan Chronicle* and a Telugu local daily *Visakha Samacharam*, evaluation of the respondent is not done (See Table 94).

Table–93
Frequency of Evaluation of Work by Management

Frequency of Evaluation	*f*	%
Every month	54	52.4
For two months	5	4.9
Every quarter	25	24.3
Once in a year	19	18.4
Total	**103**	**100**

Table–94
Frequency of Work Evaluation of the Respondents by Media Organization

Media Organization	*Every Month*		*Every Two Months*		*Every Quarter*		*Once a Year*	
	f	%	*f*	%	*f*	%	*f*	%
Newspaper								
Andhra Bhoomi	1	1.8	-	-	-	-	1	5.3
Andhra Jyothi	1	1.8	-	-	3	12	3	15.8
Deccan Chronicle	-	-	-	-	-	-	-	-
Economic Times	1	1.8	-	-	-	-	2	10.5

Contd...

Media Organization	*Every Month*		*Every Two Months*		*Every Quarter*		*Once a Year*	
	f	%	*f*	%	*f*	%	*f*	%
Eenadu	5	9.3	-	-	5	20	-	-
New Indian Express	1	1.8	1	20	2	8	-	-
Prajasakhti	3	5.6	-	-	-	-	1	5.3
The Hindu	5	9.3	1	20	3	12	2	10.5
Times of India	3	5.6	-	-	2	8	2	10.5
Vaartha	5	9.3	-	-	-	-	-	-
Visakha Samacharam	-	-	-	-	-	-	-	-
Visalandhra	1	1.8	-	-	2	8	1	5.3
Television Channel								
Etv	10	18.5	2	40	4	16	1	5.3
Etv2	5	9.3	-	-	1	4	-	-
Excel	-	-	-	-	1	4	-	-
TV9	6	11.1	1	20	2	8	3	15.8
Radio								
All India Radio	7	13.0	-	-	-	-	3	15.8
Total	**54**	**100**	**5**	**100**	**25**	**100**	**19**	**100**

In evaluating the work of the respondents, the Chi square analysis did not differ significantly among the media organizations ($X^2 = 0.0008$, $p < 0.5$, $df = 48$). It is also interesting to note that the methods adopted for evaluation. The methods of evaluation of the respondents in each organization are different. However, respondents reported four methods such as 1. Number of stories 2. Examination 3. Ranking and 4. Others. The evaluation of the performance of the reporters is done in terms of stories filed by them. While in the case of copy editors, examinations are conducted. In the case of producers, the total number of programmes produced in a given period is taken into consideration for ranking (Table 95).

Table-95
Ways of Work Evaluation of the Respondents by Media Organization

Media Organization	*Stories*		*Exams*		*Ranking*		*Others*	
	f	%	*f*	%	*f*	%	*f*	%
Newspaper								
Andhra Bhoomi	-	-	-	-	1	10	1	2.1
Andhra Jyothi	2	4.7	1	50	-	-	4	8.3
Deccan Chronicle	-	-	-	-	-	-	-	-
Economic Times	2	4.7	-	-	-	-	1	2.1
Eenadu	4	9.3	-	-	-	-	6	12.5
New Indian Express	4	9.3	-	-	-	-	-	-
Prajasakhti	1	2.3	-	-	2	20	1	2.1
The Hindu	6	14.0	-	-	1	10	5	10.4
Times of India	5	11.6	1	50	-	-	1	2.1
Vaartha	2	4.7	-	-	1	10	2	4.2
Visakha Samacharam	-	-	-	-	-	-	-	-
Visalandhra	1	2.3	-	-	-	-	2	4.2
Television Channel								
Etv	7	16.2	-	-	2	20	8	16.7
Etv2	1	2.3	-	-	-	-	5	10.4
Excel	1	2.3	-	-	-	-	-	-
TV9	5	11.6	-	-	1	10	7	14.5
Radio								
All India Radio	2	4.7	-	-	2	20	5	10.4
Total	**43**	**100**	**2**	**100**	**10**	**100**	**48**	**100**

Transfers

With regard to transfers, only 16 (12.6%) respondents out of 127 have been transferred to different places owing to office work. Out of these 16 respondents, 14 (88.2%) of them have been transferred only once in their service (Table 96).

Table-96
Number of Transfers Obtained by Respondent During Her Career

Number of Transfers	*f*	%
Once	14	88.2
Twice	1	5.9
More than two times	1	5.9
Total	**16**	**100**

Work for Outsiders

Are these respondents allowed to work for outsiders? Only 16.5 per cent of the total respondents reported that they are allowed to work for outsiders and these respondents are on contract employment with the organization. Mostly, these respondents are freelancing for other organization (Table 97).

Table-97
Type of Work Outside the Office

Type of Work	*f*	%
Freelancing	10	47.6
Temporary job	2	9.5
Any other	9	42.9
Total	**21**	**100**

Change of Organization

In the career of a journalist, promotion is an aspiration of every journalist, and is also linked with job satisfaction. Rise in salary and satisfactory working conditions prompted the respondents to change organizations. Out of the total 127 respondents, 44

(34.6%) respondents reported change of organization. Out of these 44 respondents, more (54.5%) than half of them changed the organization only once while 27.3 per cent of them changed the organizations twice. Interestingly one respondent changed the organization for five times during the career (Table 98). The one respondent is from *Andhra Jyothi.*

Table–98
Number of Organizations Changed by the Respondent

Number of Organizations Changed	*f*	%
One	24	54.5
Two	12	27.3
Three	5	11.4
More than three	2	4.5
Five	1	2.3
Total	**44**	**100**

Further inquiry revealed the reason for the change in the organization. Most of (38.6%) them reported better pay was the reason for change of organization. About 20 per cent of them cited other reasons for changing the organizations, followed by 18.2 per cent respondents who reported better working condition was the reason for changing organizations. About 20 per cent of the respondents cited promotion, job security and inability to cope with superiors (Table 99).

Table–99
Reasons for Changing from Previous Organization

Reason for Change	*f*	%
Promotion	3	6.8
Better pay	17	38.6
Working conditions	8	18.2
Job security	3	6.8

Contd...

Reason for Change	*f*	%
Unable to cope with superior	3	6.8
Organization was too small	1	2.3
Others	9	20.5
Total	**44**	**100.0**

N = 127

Job Expectations

The researchers asked a specific question related to job that whether the job was meeting their expectations. Over 60 per cent responded by saying that the "job meets their expectations, while 11 per cent informed that the job exceeded their expectations. However, 28 per cent of them reported that the job had not met their expectations (Table 100). A majority of these respondents belong to *The Hindu* (24.9%), followed by *Etv* (3.8%) and *Etv2* (13.8%) (See Table 101).

Table-100
Extent of Job Meeting the Expectations

Job Expectation	*f*	%
It meets the expectations	77	60.6
It exceeds the expectations	14	11.0
Has not met the expectations	36	28.4
Total	**127**	**100**

The chi square analysis did not differ significantly in terms of meeting expectations of respondents from organizations. ($x^2 = 0.0008$, $p< 0.5$, $df = 48$). Nevertheless a particular question was asked whether the respondents wanted to continue in the present job. As much as 88 per cent of them want to continue in the present job.

About 53 per cent wanted to work somewhere other than media, while one respondent wanted to work in the government (Table 102). Despite these reasons the researcher

Table-101
Respondent's Expectations of the Job from Different Media Organizations

Media Organization	*Job Meeting the Expectations*		
	It Meets Expectations (n = 77)	*It Exceeds my Expectations (n = 14)*	*It Hasn't Met Expectations (n = 36)*
	%	%	%
Newspaper			
Andhra Bhoomi	1.29	-	2.8
Andhra Jyothi	9.03	-	2.8
Deccan Chronicle	3.87	-	-
Economic Times	3.87	-	
Eenadu	11.61	7.14	2.8
New Indian Express	5.16	-	-
Prajasakhti	6.49	14.28	2.8
The Hindu	7.74	-	24.9
Times of India	9.03	-	2.8
Vaartha	3.87	7.14	11.2
Visakha Samacharam	-	-	2.8
Visalandhra	7.74	-	-
Television Channel			
Etv	10.32	35.7	13.8
Etv2	1.29	7.14	13.8
Excel	1.29	-	-
TV9	10.32	14.28	11.2
Radio			
All India Radio	6.49	14.28	8.3
Total	**100.0**	**100.0**	**100.0**

proposed to examine the major complaint with the job. The respondents accorded different answers. Out of 127 respondents, 48 per cent of them did not have any complaint about the job (Table 103). But, 79 of them expressed different problems (Table 103). Some of them are; lack of time to do good job (15.2%), salary (15.2%), odd working hours (11.4%), lack of opportunity to write or be creative (10.1%).

Table-102
Respondent's Preference to Work other than the Present Job

Respondent's Preference	*f*	%
Other newspaper	2	11.8
Government	1	5.9
Television	4	23.5
Public Relations	2	11.8
Others	8	47.0
Total	**17**	**100**

Table-103
Major Complaint with the Present Job

Major Complaint	*f*	%
Lack of time to do good job	12	15.2
Salary	12	15.2
Odd working hours/shift	9	11.4
Lack of opportunity to write/to be creative	8	10.1
Allotment of work against my subject/interest	7	8.8
Lack of encouragement to do good job	7	8.8
Job security	6	7.6
Low staff morale	6	7.6
Indifferent attitude of superior	4	5.1

Contd...

Major Complaint	*f*	*%*
Lack of social life	4	5.1
Lack of promotional avenues	3	3.8
News room lacks feasible policy	1	1.3
Total	**79**	**100.0**

Lastly, the question was asked whether they wanted their children to continue in the present job. Only 23.6 per cent of them wanted their children to continue in the profession, while, 20.5 per cent did not want their children to join in the profession. However, about 56 per cent could not express their view to this question (See Table 104).

Table-104
Respondent's Perception of Her Child to Take Up Media Job: Media-wise

Media Organization	*Yes*	
	f	*%*
Newspaper		
Andhra Bhoomi	-	-
Andhra Jyothi	-	-
Deccan Chronicle	-	-
Economic Times	1	3.3
Eenadu	2	6.7
New Indian Express	1	3.3
Prajasakhti	3	10.0
The Hindu	2	6.7
Times of India	2	6.7
Vaartha	-	-
Visakha Samacharam	-	-

Contd...

Media Organization	*Yes*	
	f	%
Visalandhra	-	-
Television Channel		
Etv	8	26.7
Etv2	2	6.7
Excel	-	-
TV9	5	16.7
Radio		
All India Radio	4	13.2
Total	**30**	**100**

7

CASE STUDIES

Although the earlier chapters have presented quantitative data related to the personal, family including spouse, work environment, and job satisfaction of the respondent, a detailed examination of certain other issues has not been possible in the quantitative study. Thus, the present chapter presents four case studies of working media women who have figured in the sample. Further, the case studies make an attempt to supplement the quantitative data with additional information about the personal, professional and organizational aspects that these working media women come across in their career.

Case Study 1

Ms. S. aged 39 has started her career in 1991 as radio compeer for *yuva vani* programme on All India Radio on a contract basis. She evinced interest on the media job when she heard that AIR station had advertised for the post of a radio announcer. Through audition, she was selected for the post, and she continued it till 1993. Because of her marriage in 1993, she discontinued the job. She waited for more than two years to take up another job. In 1995, she was selected as a casual announcer for AIR station in the same place where she was working earlier as a radio compeer. Encouraged by her husband, she took up a career in a local cable network as a news reader on a paltry sum of Rs. 100 for each news bulletin. She was given 12 news bulletins in a month. In view of the low amount she was receiving from the cable network, she continued as a casual announcer in the radio. Though she was married in 1993; she lost her husband in five years when she gave a birth to a female child. With the loss of a life partner, she had to shoulder the responsibility of the family and to educate her daughter. Without much support from her in-laws and her own parents, she decided to work in the media organization as she was familiar with the nature of the work. In order to earn more money for the sustenance of herself and her daughter, she had to work hard. Later, her position as a news reader was upgraded in the cable network as a staff reporter to give her more salary while she was allowed to work as a casual announcer in All India Radio. Though she obtained satisfaction in the job, she had to cope with the employment in spite of odd working hours. In the local television reporting, she was given soft beats like press conferences and seminars. The view of the management was that Ms. S. "being a woman" could not be given crime or political reporting. On the other hand, she could not spend time with her daughter as Ms. S. was away from home from the morning to late evening. By the time she reached home, the child was going to sleep. Her daughter used to complain that her mother was "busy with news reading." Although the job was strenuous, it used to give her satisfaction because she was appearing on the screen.

While working in the cable news network, she completed her master's degree in journalism and mass communication in 2001. Because of her academic qualification in journalism and mass communication, she was confident of working as a news reporter.

Ms. S. says that sympathy as a widow helped her in getting the job as a staff reporter. Nevertheless, she resigned the job as a news reporter to join *ETV* as a programme associate in 2003. She shifted from one city to another city, leaving behind her daughter with her parents. Although she got an increase in her salary, she was constantly reminded of her child, and leaving her child with her parents was painful. Because of her daughter and other family problems, she had to resign her job in *ETV* to come to her native city to join as a public relations officer in police department in 2007. For a period of one year, she worked in the police department. Initially, she was afraid to work in the male-dominated department. She could not work in the department with satisfaction because of the bureaucratic environment and also with the frequent intrusion of media people into her work. Above all, the job in the police department was strenuous and she could not keep her bosses happy. She was constantly haunted by the thoughts of losing the job because of mounting pressure on her in relation to the job such as getting good image of the police in the media. Added to it, salary was given irregularly for two or three months. Further, the nature of the duty was not specifically described to her, and she was frequently disturbed with phone calls to attend to the duty in order to send news to the media. When she wanted to spend time with her daughter, she was asked to attend to the duty. Mostly, she had to forego her weekly-off. In view of these problems, she decided to leave her job, and unexpectedly, the post of the public relations officer in the department was rescinded by the government. Then, she joined a satellite television channel as a staff reporter in 2008. In terms of salary, Ms. S. was comfortable; she did not have satisfaction in the job at present. She complains that she does not have job security. In the profession, the unprofessional approach of her colleagues, the work environment is being "disturbed", resulting in "psychological stress." Because of 24×7 news channel, she has to work more than 12 hours in sending news reports. However, she expressed the view that she is not happy with the present job. She explains that the there is no recognition for hard work in the profession while the salary is not so encouraging. Although she has never faced any problem in relation to harassment from her male colleagues, the nature of working hours pose a big problem in the profession of journalism.

Specifically, she points out that she will not allow her daughter to take up journalism job as there is "no security" in the job. This apart, she feels that the job lacks financial support in the event of a crisis. In particular, health problems persist, and lingering ill-health is increasingly becoming a problem in the profession. Nevertheless, she opines that women must come forward to work in the profession of journalism to understand the nuances of society.

Case Study 2

Ms. P. a senior copy editor in national english daily, has started her career in 1992 as a trainee journalist in Vijayawada. Inspired by her uncle who was a senior editor in a national daily, she chose to join the profession. Initially, she was given the post as a trainee copy editor with a promise that she would be transferred to a place of her choice, Hyderabad. As the management did not keep up the promise, she resigned the job to go back to her place, Hyderabad. Subsequently, she joined an evening daily in 1993. While working in the evening daily, she completed her post-graduation in political science. She worked in the evening daily for a period of two years, and found the salary was low. In 1995, she decided to join another daily which was supposed to be launched in a year. However, the daily was not launched, and the employees were asked to opt out of the organization. Meanwhile, she was married to a charted accountant in the same year. Because of the marriage, she had to shift to another city in Andhra Pradesh. She started her career again as a journalist in English daily, on being encouraged by her husband and in-laws. She worked in that english daily for two more years, and the advanced pregnancy made her quit the newspaper. When she was working in this newspaper, shift duty became increasingly "problematic" because the organization did not make any arrangements for travel from the office to home. Newspapers did away with 3-shift pattern and all employees were asked to work in two shifts. Women journalists were asked to work from 4pm to 11pm or beyond. In the absence of proper transport from the remote location of the office to the house posed a problem to the women journalists. Ms. P. had one such experience while she was returning home after 11pm. Some of the men in the nearby locality chased her and she had to run to the nearby petrol bunk to call her husband. In the late 90s mobile phones were not in operation. However, the job gave her satisfaction as she was writing special stories on the city's problems. She got an opportunity to interact with celebrities in India like S.P. Balasubramaniam (film singer), Shabna Azmi (Hindi film actress). Later, she resigned from the newspaper owing to the "delivery" of twins. She was on 'stay put" for one year without any job. During this period, she was free-lancing to *The Hindu* week-end supplement. In 2001, she was editing the industrial fortnightly as she wanted to be in the profession that is familiar to her. But, the stint in the industrial fortnightly was not satisfactory. One, she was underpaid, and second, she was not very much familiar with the subject. In 2006, she joined national english daily as a copy editor. She feels that she is happy with the job and the work environment. In terms of salary, she is drawing a comfortable amount. Moreover, the nature of the duty is 5pm to 12.30 pm in the present newspaper. She does not have to complain about the job. But, she feels that health is suffering on account of work. She frequently gets disturbed in her sleep because of late sliding into the bed. Being a woman, she has to attend to the daily chores in the house, and she gets less time to sleep. She feels newspaper organizations must provide health insurance to all the employees. Although colleagues are cooperative in the office, she claims that gender bias is shown in the office in the form of comments. She says, "Men also age, but they talk of the age of women. Male colleagues point out that the women, when they start aging, they cannot work in the office." She feels that she will not impose her ideas on her children in choosing a profession of their own. "If they choose journalism as a profession, she will not object to it."

Case Study 3

Mrs. J. aged 44 started her career in 1992 as a part-time copy editor in a vernacular daily. The reason for choosing journalism a career was that since her childhood, she had creative ideas like writing short stories and poems. Because she had the habit of writing literary pieces, she planned to become a journalist and requested one of her relatives who was working in a vernacular daily to recommend her name for a position in the same daily where he was working. Discouraged by him, she gave up the idea of becoming a journalist. However, friends encouraged her to try for a position in any vernacular newspaper. Thus, her career as a journalist began as a part-time copy editor in the newspaper.

Mrs. J. was married when she began her career. Having encouraged by her husband, she continued as a part-time copy editor for three more years till 1995. By the time she took up a job, she gave birth to two female children. As the children were young, she used to keep her in the care of her neighbours who were very cooperative. Mostly, her job was only in the evening between 4pm and 9pm. However, she could cope with the job with the utmost support given by husband and also by her neighbours. Nevertheless, she quit her job in the vernacular daily on the ground that she had a conflict with the management representatives.

Further, she joined another vernacular daily that was to be launched. In 1995, she joined the new daily to make "preparatory work" for the launch of the edition fromVisakhapatnam. In 1996, the daily was launched and her career as full-time journalist took off. Her husband being a business man used to take care of her children. As the first child was growing and taking care of the other sibling, Mrs. J. was relieved to some extent. In the profession, Mrs. J. was "sincere in working for the new daily although salary was paid irregularly." In spite of problems from the other female colleagues, she did not retreat. She continued in the profession with determination. However, she did not encounter any problems from her male colleagues. They extended her help in relation to her work and encouraged her to write on various topics. Although she was not given any promotion in spite of her seniority, she did not feel depressed nor being ignored by the management. She feels that she has a status in society and hence she derives complete satisfaction in the job. As her children have grown up, she is highly relieved from the family management. However, she had to balance between her family and profession on many occasions. Two years back, she got her elder daughter married. Having hailed from a Hindu traditional family, she was obliged to attend to many family functions owing to the marriage of her daughter. Although her husband insisted that she should attend to the functions, she fairly managed to attend to them without applying for leave in the office. On few occasions, her husband scolded her in not spending much time in the family functions.

In the beginning of her career, she showed a keen interest on writing. She wrote "inspiring articles and features" on women. She published around 40 by-line stories and received appreciation from various quarters. She feels that "professional jealousy" from her colleagues has affected her. She is not showing any interest on writing features or articles to the newspaper now-a-days. This apart, she feels strongly that she is "not recognized" in the office in spite of working hard for the newspaper in times of shortage of staff. She regrets that she is not given any incentive for working overtime in the office. Salary too is not being increased. The chief problem with the job is that the organization is not providing transport in the middle of the night, she adds.

Case Study 4

Mrs. LP has been working in ETV2 as a newsreader for the last five years. Prior to joining the present organization, she was a trainee newsreader in a private television channel which was expected to be launched in 2002. However, the news channel did not take off as expected, and Mrs. LP who was introduced to the CEO of the channel by her family friend encouraged her to take up television news reading in another channel. At that time, in response to ETV2 advertisement for news readers, she applied for the post and was selected.

Having hailed from a middle class family, she took up the job of television anchoring in a local television channel in 1999, encouraged by her father and brother who are working in the police department. With that confidence as a television anchor, she decided to be a television newsreader.

In ETV2 all newsreaders have to work in different shifts. The duration of the shift duty is eight and half hours a day. In the beginning of her career in ETV2, Mrs. LP had to work in night duty more often, "keeping a vigil on the news flow." She had to catch the breaking news and was always kept on "tenterhooks" to read the news. Because of shift duty and irregular food intake her health suffered. She suffered from jaundice which impacted her work. Since she suffered from jaundice, she was not quite often going for "night shift" as the practice in the earlier days. Although she expressed her satisfaction of the job, she claimed that the job was "highly stressful." She says that she is proud to be a newsreader although she undergoes stress in the job. Because as a news-reader she has to maintain strict regimen in the studio. She must be alert to the news and she is not expected to bungle in news reading. On many occasions she is kept on "live news", and has to coordinate and present "spot news." For instance, she says news of bomb blasts and terrorist attacks are tension ridden moments in her career. However, she says that the colleagues are cooperative and accommodative on many occasions. Since ETV2 is a big television network, she was happy to associate herself with the organization. In 2006, she got married, and her husband too was working in the same organization as a journalist. After marriage, she found her role as house wife was difficult on a few occasions. Because of the shift duty, she had to balance her career between family and job owing to the frequent visits of relatives and friends to her home.

In terms of salary, she is quite satisfied. Though she was paid Rs. 5000 in the beginning of her career, she now draws a handful of money. Nevertheless she has decided to resign from the organization for the "strict code of conduct." The job has become "routine and boring." As the other television channels are offering a good salary package, she has decided to join other organization. Lastly, she concluded that she wants her children to join the profession of journalism as she feels the jobs is challenging.

8

CONCLUSION

The proliferation of mass communication channels in India has influenced the employment trends of women and many educated women opt for a job in the mass media. During the last decade the percentage of women employment has inched up in spite of problems within the family as well as in the society. Thus, the present study has made an attempt to explore the different issues that impact women journalists and the present study specifically focuses on growing women employment in Andhra Pradesh particularly in mass media. The study specifically discusses four important issues viz., 1. caste, age and education, 2. marriage and childcare, 3. work environment and media organization, 4. job satisfaction *vis-a-vis* nature of work.

Caste, Age and Education

Caste is often examined as one of the variables in sociological studies in India as it impacts the social life. Caste plays a crucial role in society in the social interactions. It helps an individual to better her/his life and it may deprive her/him an opportunity. Therefore, the present study has made an attempt to ascertain the respondents' background in the profession of journalism or media. In the study it was found out that 89 per cent of the respondents belong to open category (OC) while 10 per cent of the respondents are from backward caste. Obviously, majority of the respondents from the open category are increasingly opting for a job in private sector because of the increasing number of jobs that are available for those with education and motivation to take up a job in the private sector. In 1990s India witnessed a fundamental shift from Nehruvian socialist style to a free market policy in which the country opened its borders to foreign investment and foreign consumer products.

Thus, in the process, the role of the government had shrunk in the economy, and laissez-fair policies prevailed (Singhal and Rogers, 2001: 45). Because of the opening of the Indian economy there is a proliferation of television networks in 1990s, and nearly 300 television channels have been launched in the country so far. In addition, the government's policy of affirmative action, government jobs are reserved for the backward caste and scheduled caste people. Because of this policy the candidates from the open category seek jobs in the private sector. Because of these reasons, more number of women seeks jobs in the media organizations which are in the private hands. The nature of media ownership is also seen as a reason for employment of open category people. Normally an open category candidate is considered to belong to the privileged section of society. Because of the market-driven forces, the recruitment policy aims at selling the media product. Vilanilam (2005) observes:

> Recruitment of media workers is also not always above board. Even in old, established newspaper organizations, young men and women belonging to the privileged sections are recruited and given in-house training aim at making them seekers of a product rather those upholders of serious socio-economic principles. Business management principles are more in application in such situations because what counts in media organizations these days is profit (p. 36).

For instance, corporate media organizations such as *Eenadu, Etv, Etv2, Deccan Chronicle, Andhra Bhoomi, Times of India, Economic Times* and *The Hindu* recruit people who are young, urbane and educated. Moreover it is also seen in the study, 54.4 per cent of the respondents are in the age group of

21-30 years. These groups of people who are young graduates work in the urban-centric and glamorous television channels. It is seen in the study that nearly half of this age group of people is working in popular and lead television channels such as *Etv2* and *TV9* which are news channels, catering to the information needs of the people in the state. *Etv2* and *TV9* which are 24×7 television channels offer jobs to the young, educated and dynamic women to work in the channels as news reporters and anchors. Furthermore, a number of universities in the country are also offering journalism programmes. It is also observed in the study that 64.6 per cent of the respondents have journalism degrees or certificates. Also, the TV networks and newspapers have in house training schools for the young people. Thus the educated women from the open category choose these jobs as compared to other castes.

Marriage and Childcare

In the study, it is found out more than half (51.1%) of the respondents earn less than Rs. one lakh per annum. Out of which, 41 per cent are earning between Rs. 50,000 to one lakh, and therefore, their monthly average income is Rs. 8,000. With the rising standard of living dual earner families (both the spouses are working) are growing. It is seen in the study that most of the respondents' spouses are working in the private sector, earning less that Rs. 1.5 lakh per annum. It is evident that 40 per cent of the respondents' spouses are earning less than Rs. 12,000 per month. On the other hand nearly 60 per cent of those married got married between 21-25 years bearing one child or two. Further, those 41 who joined job after marriage obtained husband's consent for job. Although dual earner families are emerging, the married respondents are having only one child and even in those cases where second child is there, the gap between the first and second child is more than 3 years. In the analysis more than half of them weren't completely satisfied with the childcare arrangements. Despite knowing the nature of the job the women respondents came forward to work in the media organizations where the nature of the work involved shift duty. Because of the nature of the duty, the respondents expressed the view during the data collection, that their family life is being affected in terms of recreation, childcare and so on. Out of the total 127 respondents, 11.8 per cent of the respondents avail of leave to attend children's work and 8.7 per cent of them for recreation. Nearly 24 per cent of them avail of leave to attend family or relatives functions.

It is evident from the four case studies that women journalists in specific find the jobs difficult as they face problems in relation to the family. In particular, women who have young children are increasingly facing problems. It is also seen from the case studies that the women journalists suffer from health disorders in view of the shift pattern of work, and lack of health insurance is a problem. Further, the news organization does not provide transport after the night shifts, the women journalists are exposed to the risk as seen in case study 2. However, the women in the electronic media do undergo stress in relation to the nature of job, it impacts their family relations. Unless the life partner is sympathetic to the problems, the career of the women journalists is bound to be affected.

Workplace Environment and Media Organizations

A conducive environment at the workplace encourages the employees to work effectively and promotes a harmonious understanding among peers. In the present study it is found out 78.7 per cent of the respondents joined the job between 20 and 25 years. Since the majority of the respondents joined the job in the early 20s, they were sent out on regular duty as soon as they completed in-house training given by the respective organizations. In the study sample, 35 (27.5%) respondents are working as reporters who are given different beats. Normally Indian studies have pointed out that women journalists are given "soft" beats such as education, entertainment, fashions and so on as is discussed in chapter 1. Contrary to that understanding it is found in the present study, women are given male dominated beats such as automobiles, crime, politics and business. Mostly, these beats or assignments are given to women journalists in television networks, particularly *TV9*, an aggressive 3-year old TV channel. However, other channels or newspapers have confined the women journalists to soft subjects. As observed in job model, women are assumed to perform as men to the extent that their organizational experiences are similar. In the present study, women reporters have proved that, they can also do the beats done by men.

In relation to shift duty, working women in 1970s and 1980s were not allowed to work beyond 5pm and even women workers refused to work even late hours in the office. But, such perception is radically undergoing change and in the study more than half (54.2%) of the respondents work in the night shift. Further 87.4 per cent of the respondents reported working extra hours, although some organizations do not pay for the extra work. One important failure on the part of organizations is that they don't provide childcare arrangements at the workplace. However, working media women who have children are making alternative arrangements for the childcare.

Moreover, the attitude of working women has not changed although women are expected to socialize in the organization. Nearly 50 per cent of the respondents still believe working women face problems in the office although their belief varied from "strongly believe" to "less believe." Over all, the present study found that the male colleagues treat them good and 32.3 per cent reported that their male colleagues treat them as they treat other men. Only 1.6 per cent of the respondents reported nasty behaviour and 7.9 per cent behave indifferently.

Job Satisfaction *vis-a-vis* Nature of Work

Job satisfaction is crucial for discharging duties with responsibility regardless of employment. Journalism is a creative job in which a person can render a meaningful and purposeful service if the work environment is conducive for her discharging the functions effectively. When workers job satisfaction affects the efficiency and productivity of the organization, an individual's job satisfaction will have an impact on the person's every day life and health and how long the person will remain in the job. A general view among the scholars is that journalists derive job satisfaction from tangible rewards such as salary and fringe benefits and professional rewards such as job autonomy and service to the public interest. In the present study, it was found that 69 per cent of the respondents expressed job satisfaction, while 18 per cent are very much satisfied with the job. These respondents belonged to higher income groups. Since higher salary gives them security and stability in the profession, they are very much satisfied with the job. They are from *The Hindu, Eenadu* and, *Times of India, Economic Times* and *Deccan Chronicle.* However, job satisfaction is also linked to professionalism and the freedom enjoyed in the profession. In the study, it is also found 36.3 per cent of the respondents expressed the view that opportunity to be creative is the main reason while 7.3 per cent expressed the view that salary is giving them job satisfaction. However the age and job satisfaction also showed negative correlation ($r = -0.077$), and the income and job satisfaction also negatively correlated ($r = -0.026$). The length of service and job satisfaction too showed a strong negative correlation ($r = -0.121$). On these aspects, age, income and length of service showed negative correlation with the job satisfaction. It implies that advancing age and progress in the profession are decreasing the professional satisfaction. Rather, other reasons, appreciation from peers and management gave them satisfaction. For example, *Eenadu* the largest circulated daily in the state of Andhra Pradesh recognizes the employee's creativity in the job. Moreover, the newspaper announces an incentive of giving Rs. 2000 or more for writing a good headline or bringing a scoop. The competition among the journalists in the organization for getting more incentives is one of the reasons for job satisfaction. In the study sample, it is also found that freedom in the selection of a story or angle of the story gives them satisfaction. Half of the respondents reported that they had always opportunity to report new story. Most of these respondents belonged to television networks and newspaper. Respondents from *TV9, Etv, The Hindu* and *New*

Indian Express, Times of India and *Economic Times* had the opportunity to report new story and they enjoy job satisfaction. However, very few respondents are dissatisfied with job and mostly these respondents are married.

Overall, the study finds the following:

1. In the profession of media, majority of the respondents belong to open category, and the majority of the working media women are in the age group of 21-30 years.

2. Marriage and children affect the professional life of the respondents and the job also influences the bearing of children. Job and lack of proper childcare arrangements influence the working media women to plan their family life.

3. Majority of the respondents do not believe that the working media women face problems at the workplace and majority of them reported that male colleagues treat them very good.

4. Opportunity to be creative and producing matters of significance gives the journalists' job satisfaction.

5. The major complaint with the job is lack of time to search for a good job, salary and working hours.

6. Lastly, only one fourth of the respondents want their children to take up the profession of journalism.

The study found that majority of the respondents did not express satisfaction with childcare arrangements. Some (49%) of them reported somewhat satisfaction with the childcare arrangement. Although these respondents were not completely satisfied with the childcare arrangements they were opting for a career in journalism. Therefore, it is suggested that the women journalists can plan their career by balancing the professional life with the personal life. They can also plan their recreation to spend more time with their children and spouse to avoid disharmony in life. The present study also found that 46.5 per cent of the respondents were either on contract or appointed temporarily. Some of these employees were working in big corporate companies like *Times of India* and *Economic Times*. In fact *Times of India* was the first newspaper in the country to have started contract system of employment for journalists. Those journalists who are working on a contract system may not be satisfied with the job, it is suggested therefore that the newspapers can consider employing women journalists permanently to encourage more women to join the profession, and the media organizations can also encourage more women to take up reporting.

In the study, it is observed that women come forward to work in the night shift. However, transport is not arranged by the media organization. Hence, the media organization can ensure provision of transport to the women employees to be secure and comfortable. When examining the facilities at the workplace, it is noticed that crèche is not provided at the workplace. Since media women may take care of their children when they report to duty as soon as they complete their maternity leave, a provision of crèche at the workplace will avoid discomfort for these employees. As regards the wage boards, the study observed that some organizations do not implement wage board recommendations. Therefore, it is suggested that these organizations should ensure implementation of wage boards to encourage more number of people to join the profession. In this regard, the Central and State Governments enforce wage boards on the media organizations. Further it is also found that the women journalists differed in their perception whether women face problems at workplace. Only half of them reported that they believe women face problems at the workplace. Specifically the problems described by them were only lack of cooperation, passing of comments by peers, and extended night shift duties. Therefore, it is suggested that media organizations may offer higher incentives when the night shift duty is extended to relieve working media women from stress factors and also reduce workload. In addition, the media organizations can encourage employees to participate in weekly meetings to change the attitude of peers towards their colleagues in containing the passing of comments by peers.

Lastly, it is found that one fourth of the respondents wanted their children to join the profession. It is obvious that the profession of journalism or media working is not attracting good number of young people as compared to the jobs in the information technology etc. Because the jobs in information technology are lucrative and enduring the young are opting for those jobs. Nevertheless, with proliferation of mass communication channels there is a need for young talent to join these media organizations. The profession is increasingly creative and opportunities are aplenty. More number of people should be educated to take up a job related to the media. For this purpose, the departments of journalism and mass communication can take up the task of training the youngsters to seek employment in media industry.

Appendix–I

QUESTIONNAIRE

Women in Mass Media: A Sociological Study

I. Identification Data

1. Age:

2. Caste:
   - (a) OC
   - (b) BC
   - (c) SC
   - (d) ST

3. Religion:
   - (a) Hindu
   - (b) Muslim
   - (c) Christian
   - (d) Any other

4. Marital status:
   - (a) Married
   - (b) Unmarried
   - (c) Divorcee
   - (d) Widow
   - (e) Separated
   - (f) Any other

5. Mother tongue:

6. (a) Level of education:
   - (a) Under Graduate
   - (b) Graduate
   - (c) PG
   - (d) Any other

(*b*) Have you studied any journalism course? Yes / No

(*c*) If yes, state the course?
(*a*) Degree
(*b*) Diploma
(*c*) Certificate course

(*d*) When did you complete the course?
(*a*) Before joining the job
(*b*) After joining the job

7. Designation

8. (*a*) Income per annum
(*b*) Do you have any income from other source? (per annum)

9. Present place of working

10. Native place

11. Have you migrated to the present place? Yes/No

12. If yes, when did you migrate to the present place?

13. State the reasons for migration

1. ....

....

2. ....

....

3. ....

....

14. Do you own any property? Yes/No

15. If yes, describe the property
(*a*) House
(*b*) Apartment
(*c*) Land
(*d*) Any other

II. ***Family Details***

16. Type of family
(*a*) Nuclear
(*b*) Joint family
(*c*) Extended family

17. Family size

Sr. No.	*Relationship with the Respondent*	*Age*	*Education*	*Job/ Business*

18. Details of spouse

Details	
Age	
Education	
Income (per annum)	
Type of employment (government or private or self employed)	

III. ***Marriage and Children***

19. *(a)* Type of marriage
   - *(a)* Arranged
   - *(b)* Love
   - *(c)* Any other

   (b) At what age did you get married (age of marriage)?

   (c) Is your marriage (considering 18yrs. as the legal age for marriage?)
   - *(a)* Timely
   - *(b)* Delayed
   - *(c)* Early

   (d) Reasons for early marriage, if it is an early marriage?

(*e*) Reasons for delayed marriage, if it is a late marriage?

(*f*) When did you join the present job?

(*a*) After the marriage
(*b*) Before the marriage

(*g*) If it is after the marriage, has your husband consented for taking up the job? Yes/No

20. Does your husband help you in house hold chores?

(*a*) to a great extent
(*b*) to some extent
(*c*) not at all

21. (*a*) If you have children when did you give birth to your first child?

(*a*) Before joining the job
(*b*) After joining the job

(*b*) When did you give birth to your second child?

(*c*) Reasons for the gap (if it is more than four years) please rank them.

S. No. Reasons	*Rank Order*
1. Health	
2. Professional pressure	
3. Financial constraints	
4. Child care problem	
5. Any other	

22. Parents generally depend on some people or make arrangements for care of their children. In your case have you made any such arrangements to look after your pre-school children (Ask question No. 22 to 24, when the age of the youngest child is below 14yrs). (If not applicable go to question No. 25).

(*a*) If yes, can you tell us about the type of arrangement (s) made

(*a*) Creche
(*b*) Nursery school
(*c*) Hires some one
(*d*) Care by relatives
(*e*) Help from neighbours

23. If mention of relatives is made, please note down his/her/heir relationship to you.

24. In general, will you tell us how satisfied are you with your current child care arrangements? (Circle one number below for your response).

Very much Satisfied	Some what Satisfied	Undecided
Some what dissatisfied	Very much dissatisfied	

25. *(a)* Normally employed women spend considerably less time with their children. In your case how much time do you spend with your children? (If the respondent is not married please skip the question).

    (b) Do your children help you in household chores? (If children are elderly).

    (a) Yes
    (b) No
    (c) Cannot say

26. Suppose, when your child is upset about something in the school/college, who listens and comforts the child?

    (a) Self mostly
    (b) Self and Spouse mostly
    (c) Spouse mostly
    (d) Others (specify)

27. Do you attend to all your family functions?

    (a) To a great extent
    (b) To some extent
    (c) Not at all

28. (If parents are living in the some other place...) How many times do you visit your parents? (If they are living with the respondents please skip the question).

    (a) Once in a year
    (b) Twice in a year
    (c) More than two times

29. (If in laws are living in the some other place...) How many times do you visit your in-laws in a year? (If in-laws are with the respondents please skip the question).

(a) Once in a year
(b) Twice in a year
(c) More than two times

30. (a) Working journalists have their weekly off in any week day. How do you engage your weekly off?

Sl. No.	Type of Engagement	Rank Order
1.	Cinema	
2.	Family outing	
3.	Park/beach	
4.	Get together with friends/relatives	
5.	Church/temple/mosque	
6.	Restaurant	
7.	Shopping	
8.	Any other	

(b) How frequently you go out with your husband?

(a) Never
(b) Rarely
(c) Several times a week
(d) About once a week
(e) Only on special occasions

(c) When did you last have recreation?

(d) Do you have any hobbies?

(e) Do you get time to develop them?

IV. *Work Setting*

31. What was the designation when you joined the present job?

32. Describe the type of appointment..

(a) Permanent
(b) Temporary
(c) Contract
(d) Any other

33. How did you know about the job?

    (a) Advertisement
    (b) Friends
    (c) Relatives
    (d) Any other (specify)

34. At what age did you join the present job?

35. Number of years of experience that you have gained?

36. How important are the following factors which motivated to join journalism?

Motivating Factor	*Extremely Important*	*Quite Important*	*Some what Important*	*Not Really Important*	*No Opinion*
Chance to help others/ reform the society					
Scope to express views					
Scope to move up quickly					
Unemployment/ no choice					
Recognition/power/ prestige					
Witness to history					
Salary					
To avoid monotonous jobs					
It was accidental					
Any other					

37. *(a)* Were you given formal training at the time of joining? Yes /No

    (b) If yes, what is the duration of training?

    (c) Have you been given any beat/regular duty after it?

    (d) If yes, what type of beat was given?

    (e) If yes, do you work in shifts? Yes/No

38. What are your shift timings?

(a) 10am-5pm
(b) 2-9pm
(c) 5-12pm
(d) Sometimes day and some times night shifts
(e) Complete night shift i.e., 11pm-5am
(f) No specific shift timings

39. If you work after 10pm will you be provided with the conveyance?

(a) Yes
(b) No
(c) Sometimes

40. If yes, how do you get your conveyance?

(a) On rquest
(b) On demand
(c) Self

41. (a) Do you work for extra hours? Yes/No

(b) If yes, how often do you work for more than the prescribed hours in a week?

(a) Less frequently
(b) Frequently
(c) Rarely
(d) Not at all

(c) Reasons for the extra working (rank them as 1, 2, 3....)

Sl. No. Reason	Rank Order
1. Shortage of the staff	
2. Lack of cooperation	
3. Lack of necessary inputs like stories	
4. Frequent special events	
5. Special occasions like special supplements	
6. Any other	

(*d*) Are you paid for extra hours? Yes/No

(*e*) If yes, what is the mode of payment?

(*a*) Money
(*b*) Compensatory leave
(*c*) Any other

(*f*) Do you carry your office work to your house?

(*a*) To a great extent
(*b*) To some extent
(*c*) Not at all

42. Are you paid for special assignment? Yes/No

43. Do you have the following facilities in your office?

Facilities	*Yes*	*No*	*Cannot say*
Toilets			
Drinking water			
Rest rooms			
Child care			
Canteen			
Grievance cell			
Recreation club			

44. Do you have the following additional facilities? If yes, please tick them.

(*a*) Accreditation
(*b*) Health insurance
(*c*) Any other professional membership

45. Working journalists have certain legal protections and securities apart from few privileges as part of their duty. In your case do you have the following?

(*a*) Does your management implement wage boards?

(*a*) Yes
(*b*) No
(*c*) Cannot say

(*b*) Does your management provide insurance for risk coverage?

(*a*) Yes
(*b*) No
(*c*) Cannot say

(*c*) Does your management give leave when applied?

(*a*) To a great extent
(*b*) To some extent
(*c*) Not at all

(*d*) Does your management grant you maternity leave? (Skip the question if unmarried)

(*a*) Yes
(*b*) No
(*c*) Cannot say

(*e*) How often you go on leave?

(*a*) Frequently
(*b*) Less frequently
(*c*) Rarely

(*f*) Can you state reasons for going on leave. (Please rank them).

Sl. No. Reason	*Rank Order*
1. Sickness	
2. For children	
3. Festivals	
4. Family or relatives functions	
5. Recreation	

V. *Work Environment*

46. (*a*) Please describe the working environment in your office?

(*a*) To a great extent encouraging
(*b*) To some extent encouraging
(*c*) Not at all encouraging

(*b*) What are the reasons for not at all encouraging?

47. *(a)* In a newspaper or TV channel organization you have to work with male colleagues. How do you assess the treatment you receive from male colleague at work place?

    (a) Very good
    (b) Treat us just as they treat other men
    (c) Kind and understanding
    (d) Resentful and nasty
    (e) Indifferent

48. *(a)* Do you believe working women in your office face problems?

    (a) Strongly believe
    (b) Believe
    (c) Less believe
    (d) Do not believe

    (b) If so, what type of them are they? Rank them.

Sl. No. Reason	*Rank Order*
1. Lack of cooperation	
2. Too much of work	
3. Passing of comments by peers	
4. Abuse by superiors	
5. Discrimination from management	
6. Night shift duties	
7. If any other (specify)	

VI. *Job Satisfaction*

49. How satisfied are you with the present job?

    (a) Very much satisfied
    (b) Satisfied
    (c) Dissatisfied
    (d) Very much dissatisfied
    (e) Can't say

50. What gives you greatest satisfaction in your job? (Rank them).

Sl. No.	Type of Characteristic Feature	Rank Order
1.	Producing matters of significance	
2.	Matters which make an impact	
3.	Too much of work	
4.	Opportunity to be creative	
5.	Recognition	
6.	Salary	
7.	Working with others in newsroom	
8.	If any other (specify)	

51. *(a)* Do you get appreciation for your work? Yes/No

    (b) If yes, from where do you get the appreciation?

    (a) From management
    (b) From colleagues
    (c) From readers

    (c) If no, describe the reasons?

52. *(a)* During your career have you got promotion? Yes/No

    (b) If yes, how many times have you got promotion?

    (c) If yes, tell us the reasons?

    (d) If no, what are the reasons?

53. If you have any story idea how often you get to report/write (If you work on desk please move to next question)?

    (a) Always
    (b) Very often
    (c) Rarely
    (d) Never

54. How much freedom do you usually have in deciding which aspect/angle of the story to be emphasized?

    (a) Almost complete freedom
    (b) A great deal very often
    (c) Some what
    (d) None

55. *(a)* Is your work evaluated frequently?

    (a) Yes
    (b) No
    (c) Sometimes

    (b) How frequently it is done?

    (a) Every month
    (b) For two months
    (c) Every quarter
    (d) Once in a year

    (c) What are the means of evaluation?

    (a) Number of stories
    (b) Conduct any
    (c) Examination
    (c) Ranking system
    (d) Other

56. *(a)* Were you ever transferred? Yes/No

    (b) How many times were you transferred?

    (a) Once
    (b) Twice
    (c) More than two times
    (d) None

57. *(a)* Are you allowed to work with outsiders? Yes/No

    (b) If yes, what type of work?

    (a) Freelancing
    (b) Temporary job
    (c) Any other

58. What was your major complaint with the present job? Give rank 1, 2, 3.... 13 (1 being major and 13 minor).

Sl. No. Reason	*Rank Order*
1. Lack of time to do a good job	
2. News room lacks feasible policy	
3. Job security	
	Contd...

Sl. No.	*Reason*	*Rank Order*
4.	Lack of opportunity to write/to be creative	
5.	Low staff morale	
6.	Lack of encouragement to do good job	
7.	Salary	
8.	Lack of social life	
9.	Lack of promotional avenues	
10.	Odd working hours/shift	
11.	Indifferent attitudes of superior	
12.	Allotment of work against your subject/interest	
13.	No complaint	

59. Does your present job meet the expectations you had when took it up?

    (*a*) Yes, it meets the expectations I had
    (*b*) It exceeds my expectations
    (*c*) It has not met my expectations

60. (*a*) Did you shift from other organization previously?

    Yes/No

    (*b*) If yes, how many organizations did you work earlier?

    (*c*) State reasons for leaving the earlier paper/organization? (If more than one give ranking one being the highest).

Sl. No.	*Reason*	*Rank Order*
1.	Promotion	
2.	Better pay	
3.	Newspaper/TV organization policy	
4.	Working conditions	
5.	Job security	
6.	Inability to get on with superior	
7.	Organization was too small	
8.	Others	

(d) Do you wish to continue in their profession? Yes/ No

(e) If no, where do you prefer to work?

(a) Other newspaper
(b) Government
(c) Television
(d) PR cell
(e) Others

(f) Would you like your son/ daughter to take up this profession in future?

(a) Yes
(b) No
(c) Cannot say

61. Any other information

Time :

Date :

Place :

Name of the Investigator

Appendix–II

NOTE ON STEM AND LEAF DISPLAY

This is a very useful kind of data tabulation, the exploratory technique of which was suggested by John Tukey (1977). This procedure helps us to have a sense of both the range of the data and the nature of the distribution of the data within that range.

With a stem and leaf, unlike the grouped data in class intervals, there is no loss of information regarding the individual observations themselves and the data are recoverable. Next, it helps to have some pictorial representation of the data. It is also useful to arrive at some numerical summaries of the data, such as medium, interquartile range and standard deviation (Kidder, 1981: 317).

An example displayed is obtained this way. The first step is to examine the data and pick out the high and low values that figure in the data. In the present case, the age of the respondents ranges from 21 to 59. Here the researcher decided to use 10 as the stem, since the stem and leaf display thus obtained would be particularly revealing as regards the distribution of the data values. Therefore, the 10's place is selected as a good stem and these numbers are written up from 5, to the lowest number at the bottom with lines drawn to the right of them. Now, actual data values are added as leaves along the lines right to the stem.

5

4

3

2 1 2 333

For instance, the age of five respondents was given as 21, 22, 23, 23, 23. Using 10's place as the leaf, the researcher wrote, next to the "2"to the right of the line, 1 2 333 which represent the age of respondents as 21, 22, 23, 23, 23. In this manner, all the 127 leaves are added. If a particular stem does not have data values; the stem values are not represented. However, one basic rule is that at least four stems should have leaves. Next, the leaves i.e., the numerical values of each stem are arranged in ascending order from left to right (e.g.1 2 3 3 3). The table thus obtained is called as a "cleaned" stem and leaf display (Devi Prasad, 1989).

Bibliography

Agarwal, H. (1995). *Society, Culture and Mass Communication: Sociology of Journalism.* Jaipur: Rawat Publications.

Ahmar, T. (2004). Gender and Media in South Asia, A Workshop held in Kathmandu on June 26-27. *www.southasianmedia.net.*

Aldous, E. (1982). *Two Pay Checks – Life in Dual Earner Families,* New Delhi: Sage Publications.

Altheide, D.L. (1976). *Creating Reality,* Beverly Hills, CA: Sage.

Aven, F.F., Parker, B., and McEvoy, G.M. (1993). Gender and Attitudinal Commitment to Organizations. A meta-analysis. *Journal of Business Research,* 26, 63-73.

Balasubramanya, A.S. (2005). Journalists in India: A Study of their Background, Attitudes and Professional Problems, *Karnataka University Journal of Communication,* 3:42-52.

Banerjee, N. (1989). Trends in Women Employment: Some Macro Level Observations, *Economic and Political Weekly,* 24 (17): 10-20.

Beam, R.A. (2006). Organizational Goals and Priorities and the Job Satisfaction of U.S. Journalists, *Journalism and Mass Communication Quarterly,* 83 (1): 169-185.

Beasley, M. (1989). Newspapers: Is there a New Majority Defining News? In P.Creedon (Ed.) *Women in Mass Communication* (pp. 180-194). Newsbury Park, CA: Sage.

Beasly, M.H. and Theus, K.T. (1988). *The New Majority: A Look at What the Preponderance of Women in Journalism Education Means to the Schools and to the Profession.* Lanham, MD: University Press of America.

Berk, S.F. (1985). *The Gender Factors: The Appointment of American Households*. New York: Plenum.

Berkowitz, D. (1993, winter). Work Roles and News Selection in Local TV: Examining the Business - Journalistic Dialectic, *Journal of Broadcasting and Electronic Media*, 37.

Bertz, M. and O'Connell, L. (1989). Work Orientations of Males and Females. Exploring the Gender Socialization Approach. *Sociological Inquiry*, 59, 318 - 330.

Bhavani, V.D. and Vijaya Lakshmi, P. (2005). Status of Working Women Journalists: A Study in Andhra Pradesh, *Karnataka University Journal of Communication*, 3:19-41.

Billings, M. and Moos, C. (1982). Work Stress and Stress Buffering Roles of Workers and Family Resources, *Journal of Occupational Behaviours*, 3 (2), 215 - 232.

Bledsoe, M. and Isingo-Abanihe (1989). Strategies of Child Fosterage among Manda Grannies in Sierra Leone in RJ Lesthaeghe (ed.) *Reproduction and Social Organization in Sub-Saharan Africa*, (pp. 442- 474), Berkley University: California Press.

Carroll, B. (1973). Job Satisfaction: A Review of the Literature, Ithaca, NY: New York State School of Industrial and Labour Relations, Cornell University.

Chakrabarthy, K. (1978). *The Conflictious, The Influencing World's Working Mothers*, Calcutta: Progressive Publishers.

Chambers, D., Steiner, L. and Fleming, C.(2004). *Women and Journalism* London: Routledge.

Chan, J.M., Pan, Z., Lee F.L.F., (2004). Professional Aspirations and Job Satisfaction: Chinese Journalists at Time of Change in the Media. *Journalism and Mass Communication Quarterly*, 81(2):255-273.

Chen, C., Zhu, J.H., and Wu, W. (1998) The Chinese Journalist. In David H. Weaver (ed.) *The Global Journalist*, (pp. 9-30), (ed.) David H. Weaver, NJ: Hampton Press.

Cook, E.P. (1993). The Gendered Context Life: Implications for

Women's and Men's Career-life Plans. *Career Development Quarterly*, 41, 227-237.

Cooper, A.M. (1988). *Television's Invisible Women: A five-nation Study of Anchors, Reporters and Correspondents*. Paper Presented to the AEJMC, Portland, OR.

Cott, N. (1987). *The Grounding of Modern Feminism*, New Haven: Yale University Press.

Crouter, A.C., Perry, J., Houston, M.T.L. and Crawford, D.W. (1989). The Influence of Work Induced Psychological Status on Behaviour at Home. *Basic and Applied Social Psychology*, 10(2), 273-292.

Daniels, G.L., and Hollifield, C.A., (2002). Times of Turmoil: Short and Long Term Effects of Organizational Change on Newsroom Employees, *Journalism and Mass Communication Quarterly*, 79(3): 661-680.

Demers, D.P. (1994). Effect of Organizational Size on Job Satisfaction of Top Editors at U.S. Dailies, *Journalism and Mass Communication Quarterly*, 71(4).

Devi, I.M. (1987). *Women Education Employment and Family Living: A Study of Emerging Hindu Wives in Urban India*, Delhi: Gian Publishing House.

Deviprasad, B. (1989). Dowry Victimization– A Content Analysis of News in Selected Newspapers. An Occasional Paper.

Deviprasad, B. (1996, March) Urban Family: Contemporary Patterns and Trends, Paper Presented at the Workshop on Challenges to the Urban Family: Department of Social Work, AU, Visakhapatnam.

Dodd-McCue, D. and Wright, G.B. (1996). Men, Women and Attitudinal Commitment: The Effects of Workplace Experiences and Socialization. *Human Relations*, *49*: 1065– 1091.

Dueze, M. (2003). *Journalism in the Netherlands – An Analysis of the People, the Issues and the (inter–) National Professional Environment.* www.home. pscw.uva.nl.dueze (retrieved: 30 November, 2003).

Eapen, K.E. (1967, Autumn). Daily Newspapers in India: Their Status and Problems, *Journalism Quarterly:* 520-532.

First Press Commission Report. (1954). Publication Division, Ministry of Information and Broadcasting, Government of India, New Delhi.

Flatow, G. (1994). Sexual Harassment in Indiana Daily Newspapers. *Newspaper Research Journal,* 15(3), 32-45.

Flexner, E. (1975). *Century of Struggle: The Women's Rights Movement in the United States,* Cambridge, MA: Harvard University/Press.

Gallagher, M. (1981). *Unequal Opportunities: The Case of Women and the Media.* Paris: UNESCO.

Gallagher, M. (1995). *An Unfinished Story: Gender Pattern in Media Employment,* Paris: UNESCO.

Ghadially, R. (1988). *Women in Indian Society,* New Delhi: Sage Publications.

Gitlin, T. (1983). *Inside Prime Time,* NewYork: Pantheon.

Goldscheider, A. and Waite, C. (1991). *New Families, No Families? The Transformation of the American Home.* Berkley University, California Press.

Goodrick, E.T. (1989, August). *A Comparison of Women and Men in Editorial Page Staffs.* Paper presented at the annual convention of the Association for Education in Journalism and Mass Communication, Washington DC.

Grant, J. (1988, Winter). Women as Managers: What they can Offer to Organizations? *Organisational Dynamics,* 17, 56- 63.

Henningham, J.(1990). Is Journalism a Profession? In J. Henningham (ed.) *Issues in Australian Journalism,* Melbourne: Longman Cheshire.

Henningham, J. (1996). Australian Journalist's Professional and Ethical Values, *Journalism and Mass Communication Quarterly,* 73(1): 206-218.

Herzberg, F., Bernard, M., and Barbara, S. (1959). *The Motivation to Work,* New York: Wiley.

Hickey, N. (2001, September/October). Moral Matters: Low and Getting Lower. *Columbia Journalism Review.*

Holmes, J. and Stubbe, M. (2003). Feminine Workplaces: Stereotype and Reality. In J. Holmes and M. Meyerhoff (eds.), *The Handbook of Language and Gender* (pp. 573-599). Malden, MA; Oxford.

ILO (2002). ILO Database Estimates and Projections of the Economically Active Population 1950-2010: and the United Nations World's Women: Trends and Statistics, 2000.

Inamdar, N.R. (2003). Growth of Online Newspapers and their Implications on Print Media: A Study. *A Master's Degree Dissertation, Department of Mass Communication and Journalism,* Karnataka University, Dharwad.

Jeffrey, R. (2000). *India's Newspaper Revolution: Capitalism, Politics and the Indian Language Press,* 1977-99, New Delhi: Oxford.

Jha, U.S. and Pujari, P.(eds.). 1996. *Indian Women Today: Tradition, Modernity and Challenge,* NewDelhi: Kanishka Publishers.

Johnstone, J.W.C., Slawski, E. J. and Bowman, W.W. (1976). *The News People: A Sociological Portrait of American Journalists and their Work.* Urbana: University of Illinois Press.

Joseph, A. (ed.) (1994). *Whose News? The Media and Women's Issues,* New Delhi: Sage Publications.

Kalleberg, A. (1974, February). Work Values and Job Rewards: A Theory of Job Satisfaction, *American Sociological Review,* 42.

Kaul, M. (2004, July). Raw Deal for Women Journalists, *www.indiatogether.org.*

Kidder, L.H. (1981). *Research Methods in Social Relations* (4th edition). New Delhi: Holy, Rinehart and Winston.

Kingston, P.W. and Nack. S.L. (1987). Time Together Among Dual Career Couples. *American Sociological Review,* 52 (2): 391–400.

Kinnier, R.T., Katz, E.C., and Berry, M.A. (1991). Successful

Resolutions to the Career–Versus–Family Conflict. *Journal of Counseling and Development*, 2, 152 - 177.

Kohli, V. (2006). *Indian Media Business,* (Second edition), New Delhi: Sage Publications.

Kossan, P. (1992, April - May). Sexual Harassment in the Newsroom and on the Job, *APME News,* 195 :1-11.

Lafky, S.A. (1991). Women Journalists. In Weaver, D.H. and Wilhoit, (eds.), *The American Journalists: A Portrait of US. News People and Their Work (2nd ed.)* (pp.160-181). Bloomington: Indiana University Press.

Lumsden, L. (1995). You're a Tough Guy, Mary–And a First Rate Newspaper–man: Gender and Women Journalists in the 1920s and 1930s, *Journalism and Mass Communication Quarterly, 72*(4): 913-921.

Mathur, K. (2007), Human Potential: A Case Study of Female Economic Activity in India, *International Journal for Women and Gender Research,* 1 (1): 30-34.

McAdams, K. and Beasley, M.H. (1992, August). *Sexual Harassment of Washington Women Journalists: An Initial Study.* Paper Presented at the Annual Meeting of the Association for Education in Journalism and Mass Communication, Montreal, Canada.

Meesok, K. and Kyung, H.C. (2003). Quality of Life Among Government Employees, *Social Indicators Research* 62: 387-409.

Mickelson, R.A. and Smith, S.S. (1992). Education and the Struggle against Race, Class and Gender Inequality. In Margaret L. Andersen and Patricia Hill Collins (eds.) *Race, Class and Gender: An Anthology* (pp. 359-384). Belmont, CA: Wadsworth.

Miller, P. and Miller, R. (1995). The Invisible Women: Female Sports Journalists in the Workplace, *Journalism and Mass Communication Quarterly,* 72(4):883-889.

Mills, R.D. (1994). "Russia", in Looking to the Future: A Survey of Journalism Education in Central and Eastern Europe and the Former Soviet Union, *The Freedom Forum*: 66.

Mulac, A., Bradac, J. J., and Gibbons, P. (2001). Empirical Support for the Gender-as-Culture Hypothesis: An Intercultural Analysis of Male/Female Language Differences. *Human Communication Research*, 27, 121-152.

Mwesige, P. G. (2004). Disseminators, Advocates and Watchdogs: A Profile of Ugandan Journalists in the Millennium. *Journalism*, 5(1): 69-96.

Nelson, N. (1987). Rural-Urban Child Fostering Kenya: Migration Kinship Ideology, In Cho, J. Eodes (ed.) *Migrants, Workers and the Disorder* (pp. 181- 198) London: Tavistock.

Ogan, C.L., Brown, C.J. and Weaver, D.H. (1979). Characteristics of Managers of Selected U.S. Daily Newspapers. *Journalism Quarterly*, 56(4):803-809.

Pollard, G. (1995). Job Satisfaction Among News Workers: The Influence of Professionalism, Perceptions of Organizational Structure and Social Attributes, *Journalism and Mass Communication Quarterly* 72(3):682-697.

Potter, J. (1988). Media Literacy, New Delhi: Sage Publications.

Press Institute of India Report on Status of Women Journalists in Print Media in India, (2004). *Women's Link*, 10, (3).

Ramprasad, J. (2001). A Profile of Journalists in Post Independence Tanzania, *Gazette*, 63(6): 539–555.

Rapoport, R. and Rapoport, R.N. (1982). The Next Generation in Dual Earner Family Research in J. Aldous (ed.). *Two Pay Checks: Life in Dual Earner Families*, New Delhi: Sage.

Repetti, R.L. (1987). Linkages Between Work and Family Roles, *Applied Social Psychology Annual*, 7(1): 98-127.

Repetti, R.L. (1989). Effects of Daily Workload on Subsequent Behaviour During Marital Interaction: The Roles of Social Withdrawal and Spouse Support. *Journal of Personality and Social Psychology*, 57(3): 651-659.

Rextrot, B. and Shahan, P. (1987).The Family Lifecycle and Spouse Time in House Work. *Journal of Marriage and the Family*, 43(2): 941- 956.

Rima al-Shamikh. (2004). Saudi Women Journalists Battle to Overcome Hurdles. *www.newswatch.in/news.*

Rodgers, S. and Thorson, E. (2003, December). A Socialization Perspective on Male and Female Reporting. *Journal of Communication*, 658-675.

Russial, J.T. (1994, Winter). Pagination and the Newsroom: A Question of Time, *Newspaper Research Journal* 15: 91-101.

Russial, J. T. and Wanta, W. (1998). Digital Imaging Skills and Hiring and Training of Photojournalists, *Journalism and Mass Communication Quarterly*, 75 (3): 593-605.

Sathi Reddy, V. (2005). The Impact of Journalism Education on Professional Attitudes, *Karnataka University Journal of Communication*, 3: 1-18.

Saxena, T. and Thekkudan, J. (2007). Gender Mainstreaming in Organizations: Experiences from the Grassroots. *International Journal for Women and Gender Research*, 1 (1). 149-53.

Scott, J.G. (1986). A Useful Category of Historical Analysis, *The American Historical Review*, 91.

Seager, J. and Olson, A. (1986). *Women in the World: An International Atlas.* New York: Simon and Schuster.

Second Press Commission of India Report (1982). New Delhi: Government of India Publication.

Shah, N., Gothoskar, S., Gandhi, N. and Chhachhi, A. (1994, April 30). Structural Adjustments, Feminization of Labour Force and Organizational Strategies: *Economic and Political Weekly*, 39-48.

Sharma, R.K. (1990). *Journalism as a Profession in India: A Sociological Perspective*, Bombay: Media Promoters and Publishers Pvt. Ltd.

Singhal, A. and Rogers, E.M. (2001). *India's Communication Revolution: From Bullock Carts to Cyber Marts*, New Delhi: Sage Publications.

Smith, D. and Harwood, K. (1996). Women in Broadcasting. *Journal of Broadcasting*, 10(4), 339-355.

Soloski, J. (1989). News Reporting and Professionalism. Media, Culture and Society. Vol. 207-228.

Soloski, J. (1989). Sources and Channels of Local News, *Journalism Quarterly*, 66: 864-870.

Spector, P.E. (1997). *Job Satisfaction: Application, Assessment and Consequences*, Thousand Oaks, CA: Sage.

Stamm, K. and Underwood, D. (1993). "The Relationship of Job Satisfaction to Newroom Policy Changes," *Journalism Quarterly* 70 (3): 528 - 41.

Strupp, J. (2004, March). Sun Bright or Sun Lite?, *Editor and Publisher*.

Swarajya Laxmi, C. (1992). *Women at Work Insights from Indian Organization*, New Delhi, Discovery.

Terborg, J.R. (1977). Women in Management: A Research Review, *Journal of Applied Psychology, 62*, 647-664.

Tukey, J.W. (1977). Exploratory Data Analysis. *Reading Mass*: Addeison-Wesley.

UNESCO (1985). *Communication in the Service of Women: A Report on Action and Research Programmes*, 1980-1985. Paris: UNESCO.

UNESCO (1989). *World Communication Report*. Paris: UNESCO.

Usha Rai, (2003, January-March). Women-Making and Breaking News, *Vidura. 40*:(1), 15-18.

Verma, S. and Narula, M. (1998, March 9-22). Out of the Closet, *Business India*, 317- 319.

Vijaya Lakshmi and Deviprasad, B. (1999). *Challenges of Working Families; A Study of Dual and Single Earner Families in Visakhapatnam City*. Ministry of Social Justice and Empowerment, Government of India, New Delhi.

Vilanilam, J.V. (2005). *Mass Communication in India: A Sociological Perspective*, New Delhi: Sage Publications.

Voakes, P.S. (1997). *The Newspaper Journalists of the 90's*, Reston, VA: American Society of Newspaper Editors.

Voydanoff, P. (1988). Work Role Characteristics, Family Structure Demands and Work/family Conflict: *Journal of Marriage and the Family*, 50(3), 749–761.

Voydanoff, P. (1993). *Work and Family Relationships* in J.H. Braublan (ed.) *Family Relations: Challenges for the Future,* New Delhi: Sage Publications.

Vroom, V. (1964). *Work and Motivation,* New York: John Wiley and Sons.

Walsh-Childers, Kim, C. J., and Herzog, K. (1997). Outing Sexual Harassment of Women Journalists. In Shirley Biagi and Marilyn Kera–Foxworth (ed.), *Facing Difference* (pp-172-179), California: Pine Forge Press.

Ware, S. (1982). *Holding Their Own: American Women in the 1930s.* Boston: Twayne Publisher.

Wei, W., Weaver, D.H., Owen, V. and Johnson. (1996). Professional Roles of Russian and U.S. Journalists: A Comparative Study, *Journalism and Mass Communication Quarterly,* 73 (3): 534-548.

Weaver, D.H. and Wilhoit, G.L. (1997). The American Journalist in the 1990s. In Shanto Iyengar and Richard Reeves (eds.), *Do the Media Govern? Politicians, Voters, and Reporters in America.* Delhi: Sage.

Weaver, D.H., Beam, R.A., Brownlee, B.J., Voakes, P.S. and Wilhoit, G.C. (2006). In *The American Journalist in the 21st Century: US Newspapers at the Dawn of a New Millennium,* London: Routledge.

Index